The Golden Skits of
Wing-Commander Muriel Volestrangler
FRHS and Bar

The name of Wing-Commander Muriel
Volestrangler, FRHS and Bar, was a well-kept
secret until the worldwide success of *The Golden
Skits* revealed her as the *nom-de-skitte* of Terry
'John' Cleese. Terry was born in Beccles in 1919
and has had a fairly variegated career, including
spells as a wasp farmer in Kenya, a waiter at a
crematorium, a freelance probationary officer, the
Libyan Foreign Minister and six weeks breaking in
hats for T. S. Eliot. Her first collection of verse,
That's for Starters, was based on her wartime
experience bombing Dresden. She was the first
author published in the Penguin WRAF Poets
Series. However, the success of *The Zinc Skits of
Pilot-Officer M. Volestrangler, FRH* enabled her to
devote herself to full-time flying, a role she
combined with that of Chaplain to the Society of
Rear-Gunners against Dadaism. The Wing-
Commander retired in 1984 after being poisoned
by a kipper in Glastonbury. She divides her time
between Lowestoft and Nicosia, where she spent
eight months writing the 'String' Skit. In this
edition of her skits, much of the punctuation has
been substantially corrected, a testament to the
seriousness with which she regards her work.

The Golden Skits of Wing-Commander Muriel Volestrangler

FRHS and **Bar**

METHUEN

A Methuen Paperback

First published in Great Britain 1984
This paperback edition first published in 1986
Reprinted 1986
by Methuen London Ltd
11 New Fetter Lane, London EC4P 4EE
Copyright © 1984 John Cleese

Phototypeset by Wyvern Typesetting Ltd, Bristol
Printed and Bound in Great Britain
by Richard Clay (The Chaucer Press) Ltd,
Bungay, Suffolk

British Library Cataloguing in Publication Data

Cleese, John
    The golden skits of Wing-Commander Muriel
    Volestrangler, FRHS and Bar.
    I. Title
    828'.91409   PN6175

ISBN 0-413-41560-0

This collection copyright © 1984 John Cleese

Grateful acknowledgement is due to the copyright owners of
the individual sketches for permission to reprint them in this
volume: to Phython (Monty) Pictures Ltd for 'Architects Skit',
'Sheep Skit', 'Word Association Football Skit', 'Arthur "Two-
Sheds" Jackson Skit', 'Merchant Banker Skit', 'Fairly Silly
Court Skit', 'Crunchy Frog Skit', 'Argument Skit', 'Mrs Beulah
Premise and Mrs Wanda Conclusion Visit Mr and Mrs J. P.
Sartre Skit', 'Undertakers Skit', 'Cheese Shop Skit', 'Army
Protection Racket Skit', 'Ethel the Frog Skit' (copyright ©
1984 Python (Monty) Pictures Ltd); to the Monty Python
Partnership for 'Chapel Skit' (copyright © 1983 the Monty
Python Partnership); to John Cleese and Graham Chapman for
'Goat Skit', 'Top of the Form Skit', 'Bookshop Skit', 'Hearing-
Aid Skit', 'String Skit', 'Courier Skit'; to John Cleese, Tim
Brooke-Taylor and Marty Feldman for 'Shirt Shop Skit'; John
Cleese, Graham Chapman and Marty Feldman for 'Railway
Carriage Skit'; John Cleese, Marty Feldman, Graham Chapman
and Tim Brooke-Taylor for 'The Good Old Days Skit'; John
Cleese and Marty Feldman for 'Lucky Gypsy Skit'; John Cleese
and David Hatch for 'Cricket Commentators Skit'; John Cleese
for 'The Last Supper Skit', 'Regella Skit', 'Ones Skit', 'Slightly
Less Silly than the Other Court Skit Court Skit'.

Contents

Architects Skit

by MV and Graham Chapman;
'Monty Python's Flying Circus', 20 October 1970

A large posh office. Two city gents sit facing a large table at which stands Mr Tid.

Mr Tid   Well, gentlemen, we have two architectural designs for this new residential block of yours and I thought it best if the architects themselves explained the particular advantages of their designs.

There is a knock at the door.

Mr Tid   Ah! That's probably the first architect now. Come in.

Mr Wiggin enters.

Mr Tid   Mr Wiggin of Ironside and Malone.

Mr Tid sits down. Mr Wiggin walks to the table carrying a model building and puts it down.

Mr Wiggin   Good morning, gentlemen.

City Gents   Good morning.

Mr Wiggin   This is a 12-storey block combining classical neo-Georgian features with the efficiency of modern techniques. The tenants arrive here in the entrance hall and are carried along the corridor on a conveyor belt in extreme comfort, past murals depicting Mediterranean scenes, towards the rotating knives. The last twenty feet of the corridor are heavily soundproofed. The blood pours down these chutes and the mangled flesh slurps into these . . .

City Gent One   Excuse me.

Mr Wiggin   Yes?

City Gent One   Did you say 'knives'?

Mr Wiggin   Rotating knives, yes.

City Gent Two   Do I take it that you are proposing to slaughter our tenants?

Mr Wiggin   . . . Does that not fit in with your plans?

City Gent One   Not really. We asked for a simple block of flats.

Mr Wiggin   Oh. I hadn't fully divined your attitude towards the tenants. You see I mainly design slaughter houses.

City Gents   Ah.

Mr Wiggin   Pity.

City Gents   Yes.

Mr Wiggin   Mind you this is a real beaut. None of your blood caked on the walls and flesh flying out of the windows incommoding the passers-by with this one.

Mr Wiggin indicates the model.

Mr Wiggin (*confidentially*)   My life has been leading up to this.

City Gent Two   Yes and well done, but we wanted an apartment block.

Mr Wiggin   May I ask you to reconsider.

City Gents   Well . . .

Mr Wiggin   You wouldn't regret this. Think of the tourist trade.

City Gent One   I'm sorry. We want a block of flats, not an abattoir.

Mr Wiggin   . . . I see. Well, of course, this is just the sort of blinkered philistine pig ignorance I've come to expect from you non-creative garbage. You sit there on your loathesome spotty behinds squeezing blackheads, not caring a tinker's cuss for the struggling artist. You excrement, you whining hypocritical toadies with your colour TV sets and your Tony Jacklin golf clubs and your bleeding masonic secret handshakes. You wouldn't let me join, would you, you blackballing bastards. Well I wouldn't become a Freemason if you went down on your stinking knees and begged me.

City Gent Two   We're sorry you feel that way but we did want a block of flats, nice though the abattoir is.

Mr Wiggin   Oh sod the abattoir, that's not important.

Mr Wiggin dashes forward and kneels in front of them.

Mr Wiggin But if any of you could put in a word for me I'd love to be a mason. Masonry opens doors. I'd be very quiet, I was a bit on edge just now but if I were a mason I'd sit at the back and not get in anyone's way.

City Gent One (*politely*) Thank you.

Mr Wiggin . . . I've got a second-hand apron.

City Gent Two Thank you.

Mr Wiggin hurries to the door but stops there.

Mr Wiggin I nearly got in at Hendon.

City Gent One Thank you.

Mr Wiggin leaves. Mr Tid rises.

Mr Tid I'm sorry about that. Now the second architect is Mr Wymer of Wymer and Dibble.

Mr Wymer enters carrying his model with great care. He places it on the table.

Mr Wymer Good morning, gentlemen. This is a scale model of the block, 28 storeys high, with 280 apartments. It has three main lifts and two service lifts. Access would be from Dibbingley Road.

The model falls over. Mr Wymer quickly places it upright again.

Mr Wymer The structure is built on a central pillar system with . . .

The model falls over again. Mr Wymer tries to make it stand up, but as it won't, he has to hold it upright.

Mr Wymer . . . with cantilevered floors in pre-stressed steel and concrete. The dividing walls on each floor section are fixed by recessed magnalium-flanged grooves.

The bottom ten floors of the model give way and it partly collapses.

Mr Wymer By avoiding wood and timber derivatives and *all* other inflammables we have almost totally removed the risk of . . .

The model is smoking. The odd flame can be seen. Wymer looks at the city gents.

Mr Wymer . . . Frankly I think the central pillar may need strengthening.
City Gent Two Is that going to put the cost up?
Mr Wymer I'm afraid so.
City Gent Two I don't know we need worry too much about strengthening that. After all, these are not meant to be *luxury* flats.
City Gent One Absolutely. If we make sure the tenants are of light build and relatively sedentary and if the weather's on our side, I think we have a winner here.
Mr Wymer Thank you.

The model explodes.

City Gent Two I quite agree.
Mr Wymer Well, thank you both very much.

They all shake hands in a truly extraordinary way.

Cut to Mr Wiggin watching at the window. He turns to camera.

Mr Wiggin It opens doors, I'm telling you.

(Original cast: Mr Tid *Graham Chapman*; Mr Wiggin *MV*; City Gent One *Michael Palin*; City Gent Two *Terry Jones*; Mr Wymer *Eric Idle*)

Shirt Shop Skit

by MV, Tim Brooke-Taylor and Marty Feldman;
'At Last the 1948 Show', 30 October 1967

*A rather classy, old-fashioned shirt shop. A customer is
examining some shirts. The assistant, Mr Fillet, is watching.*

Customer Ah yes. This is fine. How much is it?
Fillet Sixty-nine shillings and sixpence, sir.
Customer I'll just take one please.
Fillet . . . How many?
Customer Just one.

A pause. The customer looks up.

Fillet . . . Just *one*?
Customer Yes.
Fillet (*with a hint of desperation*)   Are you *sure* you don't need more
than one, sir?
Customer Yes, really . . . I . . . er . . . really only need one.

A pause. Fillet's eyes fill with tears, but he fights them back.

Fillet Right! Just the one it is, then. Just the one.

He turns away but loses control. He grabs the customer's arm.

Fillet *Please!*
Customer What's the matter?
Fillet Please buy just two. If you don't . . . I'm *finished.*
Customer Finished?
Fillet (*suddenly gushing*)   My wife has just left me and without her
I don't have anything to live for any more, and now I've
just been told I don't sell enough shirts and I'm going to
be fired if I don't do better. Oh please, *please* help
me.

He falls to the ground and grasps the customer round his knees, sobbing.

Customer My dear fellow, I . . .
Fillet I'm sorry.

He pulls himself together in an instant and rises.

Fillet I'm sorry, that was unforgiveable of me. I don't know what came over me. I'm . . . *all right now.* OK. Just the one shirt it is then.

He takes the shirt and starts wrapping it. The customer stares.

Customer No, really, one moment . . . well, I was thinking . . . I *do* want more than one actually . . .
Fillet No, that's terribly kind of you, but you only needed one . . .
Customer No, no, silly idea popping in to buy one silly old shirt. Half a dozen, that's what I should have.
Fillet Thank you but . . . you're only trying to help me.
Customer No, really. Give me half a dozen.
Fillet No, not after the way I broke down.
Customer Broke down? You call that breaking down? You should see the way we carry on at the bank. The average person wouldn't have noticed just now, it's only that I've trained myself to be a little *extra* observant.

Fillet suddenly takes the customer's hand.

Fillet Nobody's ever been this kind to me before. Thank you.

He disappears into the bowels of the shop. The customer looks around awkwardly.

The senior sales assistant enters. His name is Mr Bosss.

Bosss Is someone serving you, sir?
Customer Yes, thank you.

He has an afterthought.

Customer And splendidly, too.

Mr Boss looks at him.

Bosss Young Fillet? ... Fair-haired boy, about five foot eight?
Customer Yes.

A pause.

Bosss ... He didn't break down again, did he?
Customer Oh, no! No, no, he seemed ... he seemed a *tiny* little bit upset ...
Bosss ... His wife left him.
Customer Yes, I know.
Bosss ... You *know*?
Customer Yes.
Bosss I see.

He takes a deep breath.

Bosss ... It's not often that a customer understands.
Customer Oh!

He tries to laugh it off.
Mr Boss comes very, very close.

Bosss It's not easy in this shop, you see. The owner's a pretty hard man.
Customer I'm sorry.
Bosss ... You know ... there's something special about you.
Customer I only came in here to buy a shirt.
Bosss Yes, but you *care*.

Fillet reappears with the six shirts. He puts them on counter.

Bosss Are those the shirts for this gentleman, Fillet?
Fillet Yes, sir.

Mr Bosss looks at the customer for some time. Then he makes up his mind.

Bosss   I think I know what I can do to express my thanks. (*He calls.*) Rogers!

Another assistant appears.

Bosss   Rogers, get the silk shirts.
Rogers   Which ones, sir?
Bosss   *The* silk shirts.

Rogers' face contorts.

Rogers   Not . . . *the* silk shirts!
Bosss   Yes!
Rogers   But, *sir* . . .
Bosss   You heard what I said, Rogers!
Rogers   Yes, but they're the Duke of Walton's, sir!
Bosss   I know that, Rogers, *get* them!
Rogers   But he's coming to collect them this afternoon, sir!
Bosss   Get them!!!
Rogers   But what are we going to tell His Grace?
Bosss   We'll have to say they're not ready yet.
Rogers   Not *ready*?! You bloody fool!! You'll get us all the sack!!!
Bosss   *Get* them!!!
Fillet (*inspired*)   Yes, *get* them, Rogers! I've had enough of this place.

Rogers, looking terrified, runs off. Mr Bosss puts his hand on Fillet's shoulder.

Bosss   Good man, Fillet.
Fillet (*even more inspired*)   I'm not taking any more of it.
Bosss (*almost as inspired*)   Neither am I. I just want to help this gentleman . . .
Customer Oh.
Bosss   . . . and then I'm going to walk out of this hell-hole with my head held high.
Fillet (*about 9.6 on the Richter inspiration scale*)   Yes, sir, *yes*!!

*Rogers reappears carrying some shirts. But he looks strangely
uncertain and skulks by the entrance to the shop's bowels. Mr
Bosss sees him.*

Bosss   Put them here, Rogers.

Rogers   You can't do this, Bosss.

Bosss   Can't I? And who's going to stop me?

Rogers   . . . I am.

Bosss   *You* are?

Rogers   Yes. You're *mad*, Bosss! You can't let him have *these*!!

Bosss   Give them to me!!

Rogers   No!!

Bosss   All right, I'll come and get them!

*Mr Bosss strides to Rogers and struggles with him. The tussle
rapidly becomes a fight. The customer runs to them.*

Customer   No, no, please! Please!!

*But Rogers is struck to the ground and Mr Bosss has the shirts.
He stands over Rogers and takes the customer by the arm.*

Bosss   This is a good man, Rogers, and I'm going to help him,
even if it's the one good thing I've ever done. It's not
too late to start a new life.

He hands the shirts to the customer.

Bosss   There are your shirts, sir.

Customer   Well, they're very nice . . .

Bosss   Please! Don't thank me. Today . . . you taught me
something.

Customer   Oh good. Er . . . how much are they?

The Bosss laughs.

Bosss   What does it *matter*? Oh, I don't know . . . ten, no . . .
five pounds each!

The customer realises that in 1967 this is a lot.

Customer Five pounds!

Rogers emits a weird howl.

Rogers   *Five* pounds!! You can't let him have them for five
pounds. They're *thirty-guinea* shirts!!

Bosss   Shut up!

Rogers   We'll all be put in prison!!

Bosss   I don't care.

*Rogers runs at the shirts, but Mr Bosss knocks him to the
ground. He turns and gives the shirts to the customer.*

Bosss   There you are. They're yours, sir. And do you know
something? I'm glad.

Customer Yes, but . . . *thirty pounds.*

Bosss   Please! Accept them.

Fillet grasps the customer.

Fillet   Yes, please.

Customer Um . . . er . . .

Fillet   Thank you.

*Unwillingly the customer produces his wallet and starts
looking in it.*

Bosss   You're a fine man.

*Rogers leaps up at Mr Bosss but is laid out. The customer hands
over the money to Mr Bosss, who takes it, throws it in the air
with a scornful laugh, and takes the customer by the hand.*

Bosss   Goodbye . . . and thanks.

Fillet follows suit.

Fillet   Yes . . . *thanks.*

The customer walks to the door, slightly dazed.

Customer Thank you for the shirts.

> *He exits.*
> *Pause.*
> *Rogers, Bosss, and Fillet join hands and dance round in a*
> *circle singing.*

Rogers, Bosss & Fillet   We sold the shirts, we sold the shirts.

> (Original cast: Customer *Graham Chapman*; Fillet *Tim*
> *Brooke-Taylor*; Bosss *MV*; Rogers *Marty Feldman*)

Goat Skit

by MV and Graham Chapman;
'The Frost Report on Crime', 8 June 1967

> *A sitting room. In the middle of the room lies a dead body,*
> *covered by a sheet. By the body stands Sergeant Ibsen. The*
> *door to the hall opens and Detective-Inspector Sophist enters*
> *the room.*

Sophist   Good afternoon, Constable. I'm Sophist of the Yard.
Ibsen   Good afternoon, sir. Sergeant Ibsen. I was asked to stay
here and give you any assistance I could, sir.
Sophist   Thank you, Sergeant. Ah, there's the body.

> *He goes to it.*

Sophist	There's a sheet over it, I see.
Ibsen	Yes, sir, we covered . . .
Sophist	Quiet, please Sergeant, I'm thinking. So . . . he was sleeping out here on the floor when he was killed.
Ibsen	No, sir, we put . . .
Sophist	Be quiet, Sergeant, don't interrupt.
Ibsen	But sir, it was us . . .
Sophist	Sergeant! . . . *please* . . . Now, why should he have been sleeping out here on the floor if this is *his* flat? Has his bed been slept in?
Ibsen	Well yes, sir, but . . .
Sophist	Thank you, Sergeant. So . . . if he spent the night out here on the floor, his bed must have been slept in by the murderer. So the murderer was obviously a friend. Now why should the friend want to spend the night in the bed?
Ibsen	Sir . . .
Sophist	I'll tell you. He required the softness of the bed because he suffered from a painful condition of the back, such as lumbago. Ah!

Inspector Sophist dashes to a picture hanging at an angle on the wall above the sofa.

Sophist	Observe this picture. It is askew. Now why should it have been moved? On purpose? Certainly not. And how could it be moved by accident – by someone brushing casually against it with his shoulder. But the picture is *above* the sofa! Are you asking me to believe that the murderer stood on the sofa?
Ibsen	No sir.
Sophist	Of course not! Clearly our man was standing in front of the sofa leaning backwards when he moved the picture. He is therefore at least . . . eight feet tall.

Inspector Sophist whips out a tape measure and checks this.

Sophist	Eight foot three inches! Now ask yourself why he should be leaning backwards in such a strange fashion? Because . . . he was looking at something, while wearing a

Guards Officer's cap. With a low peak, you see. So
every time he wanted to look at something he had to
lean backwards, like this.

He demonstrates, knocking over a lamp on the coffee table.

Sophist Hence the lumbago. What was he looking at? Obviously,
the body. Why from here? Because he was *long-sighted.*
Hence the lamp which he knocked over here.

Ibsen Er . . .

Sophist Sergeant, please – no red herrings. Now you probably
noticed the slight scratch on the lintel over the door –
the sort of scratch I recognise as that made by the cap
badge of an eight-foot-tall backwards-leaning Guards
Officer. The angle at which a man has to lean back to
see under the peak of a Guards Officer's cap is 28½
degrees. Now an eight-foot man leaning backwards at an
angle of 28½ degrees would *not* be tall enough to touch
the lintel of the door. *Unless* . . . he was *hopping* or
leaping. And why would he be hopping? Because he had
a wooden leg.

Ibsen A wooden leg, sir???

Sophist Now, where does the woman fit in?

Ibsen . . . Woman??

Sophist Cherchez la femme, Ibsen, cherchez la femme. The
woman is young – pretty – upper-class. Probably
wearing a white fur coat. *But* . . . notice the cigarette-
ends in the ash-trays . . . on none of these cigarettes is
there a trace of lipstick. Therefore, no woman.
Therefore the Guards Officer must have been wearing
the fur coat. Why was he wearing a white fur coat? To
keep his back warm because of the lumbago, Sergeant.
You see how it all fits together, Sergeant.

He returns to the body.

Sophist Now, how did this poor man meet his end?

Ibsen He was stabbed, sir.

Sophist Stabbed in the back?

Ibsen Yes sir, twice.

Sophist   Wounds about seven inches apart?
Ibsen   Yes sir.
Sophist   Just as I thought. You see, Sergeant, you will probably have noticed the carpet. It has virtually no pile, and yet it is a new carpet.

He bends down and sniffs it.

Sophist   Three weeks old, I should say. Now why should a virtually new carpet have no pile? Because the pile has been methodically and evenly removed. What has the removal of the pile of a new carpet got to do with stab wounds seven inches apart? The answer – a goat!
Ibsen   A *goat*?????
Sophist   Let us reconstruct the crime. There's a knock at the door. The murdered man answers it. It's an old friend – an eight-foot backwards-leaning Guards Officer with a wooden leg and a goat. In he hops – grazing the lintel with his cap badge. He complains of lumbago and goes to bed. The victim decides to sleep in here. In the dead of night, in hops our long-sighted friend. He stands here by the sofa leaning backwards in order to focus on his victim and accidentally moves the picture. He sees the goat nibbling the pile from the carpet, picks it up and stabs his recumbent friend in the back with it. Next, he sits on the sofa and smokes . . .

Sophist glances at the ashtray

Sophist   . . . *twenty-seven* cigarettes. Any man, Sergeant, who smokes twenty-seven cigarettes consecutively would be likely to have a very nasty cough.

There is the sound of a cough. Sophist springs to his feet and goes to a large cupboard door.

Sophist   Here's your man, Sergeant.

He flings the door open, revealing an eight-foot backwards-

leaning Guards Officer, wearing a white fur coat and carrying a bloodstained goat.

(Original cast: Sophist *Ronnie Corbett*; Ibsen *Ronnie Barker*; Eight-foot backwards-leaning Guards Officer wearing a white fur coat and carrying a bloodstained goat *MV*)

Sheep Skit

by MV and Graham Chapman;
'Monty Python's Flying Circus', 12 October 1969

The countryside. A real rustic in smock and floppy hat stands leaning on a gate. After a moment, a city gent appears and sees him.

City Gent Good afternoon.
Rustic Afternoon.
City Gent Lovely day, isn't it?
Rustic Ar, 'tis that.
City Gent . . . Are you on holiday, or . . .?
Rustic No, no, I live here.
City Gent Jolly good too.

The city gent also leans on the gate and gazes at the view. After a little time he looks puzzled.

City Gent I say – those *are* sheep, aren't they?

Rustic Ar.

City Gent Yes, of course, I thought so. Only . . . why are they up in the trees?

Rustic A fair question and one that in recent weeks has been much on my mind. It is my considered opinion that they're nesting.

City Gent Nesting?

Rustic Ar.

City Gent Like birds?

Rustic Exactly! Birds is the key to the whole problem. 'Tis my belief that these sheep are labouring under the misapprehension that they're birds. First, observe their tendency to 'op about the field on their back legs. Now . . . witness their attempts to fly from tree to tree. Notice that they do not so much fly as plummet.

There is the sound of an ovine plummet.

Rustic See the ewe in that oak tree there? She is clearly teaching 'er lamb to fly.

A long high-pitched bleat and crunch is heard.

Rustic Talk about the blind leading the blind.

City Gent Yes, but *why* do they think they're birds?

Rustic Another fair question. One thing is for sure; a sheep is not a creature of the air. It 'as appalling difficulty with the comparatively simple act of perching.

A loud baa-and-splat.

Rustic As you see. Vis-à-vis flight, its body is totally unadapted to the problems of aviation. Trouble is, sheep are dim. Once they get an idea into their heads there's no shifting it.

City Gent But where did they get the idea from?

Rustic From 'Arold. 'E's the one over there under the elm. 'Arold's that most dangerous of animals – a *bright* sheep. 'E's realised that a sheep's life consists of standing around for a bit and then being eaten. Now, that's a

depressing prospect for an ambitious sheep. So 'e's
patently 'it on the idea of escape.

City Gent Why don't you just get rid of Harold?

Rustic   Because of the enormous commercial possibilities should
'e succeed.

(Original cast: City Gent *Terry Jones*; Rustic *Graham
Chapman*)

Top of the Form Skit

(by MV and Graham Chapman; originally from 'At Last
the 1948 Show', 15 March 1967; this revised version
from the 1981 Amnesty Gala 'The Secret Policeman's
Other Ball')

The Top of the Form *Signature Tune 'Marching Strong' is
played.*

Question-master   Hello, good evening, and welcome to another
edition of *Top of the Form*. And this week we're at the
semi-final stage and tonight's contest is between the
boys of the King Arthur's Grammar School, Podmoor,
and the girls of the St Maria Kangarooboot the Second
County High School and a half.

Two seconds' frenetic recorded echoing applause.

Question-master   And so, without further ado, let's go straight on
with round two. Brian – what is the name of the meat
that we get from pigs?

Brian   Pork.

Question-master Good, that's two marks to you, Brian. Tracey –
what is the name of the metal alloy we get from zinc and
copper?

Tracey Brass.

Question-master No, I'm afraid not. The answer's pork. Kevin –
what is the capital of Australia?

Kevin Sydney?

Question-master No, no, the capital of Australia is pork. Now,
Arthura – who wrote *A Tale of Two Cities*?

Arthura . . . Pork?

Question-master Good. It's two marks to you. And so on to
Stig's question. Stig – what was the date of Captain
Cook's discovery of Australia?

Stig (*quickly*): Pork!

Question-master Good. It's two marks to you, and the last
question in this round goes to you, Cynthia. Can you
recite the first two lines of Thomas Gray's *Elegy Written
in a Country* . . .

Cynthia Pork!!

Question-master Good. Two marks to you. That's the end of
round two and the score is four points to each school.

Two seconds' applause.

Question-master And straight on to round *two*. Brian – what
is the name that we give to the meat we get from pigs?

Brian (*screaming*) Pork!!!!!

Question-master No. You're guessing, aren't you? The meat we
get from pigs is called . . . *Baghdad*. Your question next,
Tracey. What is the capital of Iraq?

Tracey Baghdad.

Question-master No. Nearly. The capital of Iraq is Rome. Kevin
– what is the capital of Italy?

Kevin . . . Paris?

Question-master No, the capital of Italy is Tokyo. Arthura –
what is the capital of Japan?

Arthura (*calculatingly*) . . . Washington?

Question-master Good!! Two marks to you. Stig, what is the
capital of the United States of America?

Stig Sydney.

Question-master   Well . . .
Brian   Canberra!
Question-master   Jolly good, two to you. And finally, Cynthia –
what's the capital of Australia?
Cynthia (*very quietly*)   Pork?
Question-master   Well done! Well done indeed!! And the score
at the end of round two is, um . . . er . . .

One second's applause.

Question-master   And on with round three. Brian – what is
the difference between a mon*soon* . . . and a mon*goose*?
Brian   A mongoose is a long white plastic pole which you hang
out of your window to frighten birds away . . . and a
monsoon is a spring-loaded medieval Hungarian
stomach pump.
Question-master   . . . No, I can only give you a half for that.
Brian   Brussels?!
Question-master   No, not Brussels. Well tried, though. No, the
answer is, a monsoon is a *wind*, and a mongoose *isn't*.
Stig – what's the capital of North Korea?
Stig   Pyong Yang.
Question-master   Yes, but I'm not giving you any points for that
because nobody likes a clever dick. So that's the end of
that round and the score is . . . um . . . is . . .

Half a second's applause.

Question-master   Now on to round four which is all about
butterflies. Tracey – your question about butterflies
is . . . who wrote *Jane Eyre*?
Tracey   Red Admiral? . . . Cabbage White? . . . Fritillary?
Question-master   No, no you're on the wrong track here.
Tracey   Pork?
Question-master   No, the answer is the Taj Mahal. No! No,
sorry, I got a bit muddled there. The answer is in fact
Brussels, but I can give you one for Cabbage White.
Now that brings the score even, and there's only time
for one more question, and whichever school gets this
question right goes into the final.

ALL   Pork! Pork!! Pork! Pork!!!!! Pork! Pork!!! Pork!!
              Pork!!!!!!!!
Question-master   No, no. No, quiet please. Here's the question.
              Ready? Who shuffled my question cards just before
              transmission?
Brian, Stig, Kevin, Arthura, Cynthia   Tracey!

The question-master bisects Tracey with a large meat cleaver.

(Cast for the Amnesty version: Question-master *MV*;
Brian *Rowan Atkinson*; Kevin *John Fortune*; Stig *Griff
Rhys-Jones*; Tracey *Tim Brooke-Taylor*, Arthura *John Bird*;
Cynthia *Graham Chapman*)

Word Association Football Skit

by MV; from gramophone record
'Monty Python's Matching Tie and Handkerchief', 1973

Man   Good evening. Tonight's the night I shall be talking
              about of flu the subject of Word Association football.
              This is a technique out a living much used in the
              practice makes perfect of psychoanalysister and brother
              and one that has occupied piper the majority rule of my
              attention squad by the right number one two three four
              the last five years to the memory. It is quite
              remarkablebakercharlie how much the miller's son this
              so-called while you were out word association
              immigrants' problems influences the manner from

heaven in which we sleekit cowerin timrous beasties all-Americal Speke the famous explorer. And the really well that is surprising partner in crime is that a Lot and his wife of the lions' feedingtime we may be c d e effectively quite unaware of the Fact or Fiction section of the Watford Public Library that we are even doing it is a far, far better thing that I do now then, now then, what's going onward Christian Barnard the famous hearty part of the lettuce now praise famous mental homes for loonies like me, at all. So on the button, my contention causing all my headaches, is that unless we take into account of Monte Christo in our thinking George V this phenomenon the other hand we shall not be able satisFact or Fiction-section of the Watford Public Libraryagainily to understand to attention when I'm talking to you and stop laughing, about human nature, man's psychological make-up some story the wife'll believe and hence the very meaning of life itselfish bastard . . .

(etc, etc, etc . . .)

Bookshop Skit

by MV and Graham Chapman;
'At Last the 1948 Show', 1 March 1967

A quite spacious bookshop. A customer enters and approaches the counter, behind which stands an assistant.

Assistant Good morning, sir.
Customer Good morning. Can you help me? Do you have a copy

	of 'Thirty Days in the Samarkand Desert with a Spoon' by A. E. J. Elliott?
Assistant	Um . . . well, we haven't got it in stock, sir.
Customer	Never mind. How about 'A Hundred and One Ways to Start a Monsoon'?
Assistant	. . . By . . .?
Customer	An Indian gentleman whose name eludes me for the moment.
Assistant	I'm sorry, I don't know the book, sir.
Customer	Not to worry, not to worry. Can you help me with 'David Copperfield'?
Assistant	Ah, yes. Dickens . . .
Customer	No.
Assistant	. . . I beg your pardon?
Customer	No, Edmund Wells.
Assistant	. . . I think you'll find Charles Dickens wrote 'David Copperfield', sir.
Customer	No, Charles Dickens wrote 'David Copperfield' with two 'p's. This is 'David Coperfield' with *one* 'p' by Edmund Wells.

Assistant (*a little sharply*)   Well in that case we don't have it.

Customer	Funny, you've got a lot of books here.
Assistant	We do have quite a lot of books here, yes, but we don't have 'David Coperfield' with one 'p' by Edmund Wells. We only have 'David Copperfield' with two 'p's by Charles Dickens.
Customer	Pity – it's more thorough than the Dickens.
Assistant	More *thorough*?
Customer	Yes . . . I wonder if it's worth having a look through all your 'David Copperfields' . . .
Assistant	I'm quite sure all our 'David Copperfields' have two 'p's.
Customer	Probably, but the first edition by Edmund Wells *also* had two 'p's. It was after that they ran into copyright difficulties.
Assistant	No, I can assure you that all our 'David Copperfields' with *two* 'p's *are* by Charles Dickens.
Customer	How about 'Grate Expectations'?
Assistant	Ah yes, we have that . . .

He goes to fetch it and returns to the counter.

Customer ... That's 'G–r–a–t–e Expectations', also by Edmund Wells.

Assistant I see. In that case, we don't have it. We don't have anything by Edmund Wells, actually – he's not very popular.

Customer Not 'Knickerless Nickleby'? That's K–n–i–c–k–e–r ...

Assistant No!

Customer Or 'Quristmas Quarol' with a Q?

Assistant No, *definitely ... not.*

Customer Sorry to trouble you.

Assistant Not at all.

Customer I wonder if you have a copy of 'Rarnaby Budge'?

Assistant (*rather loudly*) No, as I say, we're right out of Edmund Wells.

Customer No, not Edmund Wells – Charles Dikkens.

Assistant Charles Dickens?

Customer Yes.

Assistant You mean 'Barnaby Rudge'.

Customer No, 'Rarnaby Budge' by Charles Dikkens ... that's Dikkens with two 'k's, the well-known Dutch author.

Assistant No, no – we don't have 'Rarnaby Budge' by Charles Dikkens with two 'k's the well-known Dutch author, and perhaps to save time I should add right away that we don't have 'Carnaby Fudge' by Darles Tikkens, nor 'Stickwick Stapers' by Miles Pikkens with four Ms and a silent Q, why don't you try the chemist?

Customer I did. They sent me here.

Assistant (*making a mental note*) ... *Did* they?

Customer I wonder if you have ... 'The Amazing Adventures of Captain Gladys Stoat-Pamphlet and her Intrepid Spaniel Stig among the Giant Pygmies of Corsica', Volume Two.

Assistant No, we don't have *that* one. Well, I mustn't keep you standing around all day ...

Customer I wonder if ...

Assistant No, no, we haven't got it. I'm closing for lunch now anyway.

The assistant moves rapidly away from the counter.

Customer ... But I thought I saw it over there.

The assistant checks and turns slowly.

Assistant   . . . What?
Customer   Over there.

He indicates a bookshelf.

Customer   'Olsen's Standard Book of British Birds'.
Assistant (*very suspiciously*)   . . . 'Olsen's Standard Book of British Birds'?
Customer   Yes.
Assistant   . . . O–l–s–e–n?
Customer   Yes.
Assistant   B–i–r–d–s?
Customer   Yes!
Assistant   Well, we do have that one, yes.

He goes and takes the book off a shelf.

Customer   . . . The *expurgated* version, of course.
Assistant   . . . I'm sorry, I didn't quite catch that.
Customer   The expurgated version.
Assistant   The *expurgated* version of 'Olsen's Standard Book of British Birds'?
Customer   Yes. The one without the gannet.
Assistant   The one without the gannet?! They've *all* got the gannet – it's a standard bird, the gannet, it's in all the books.
Customer   Well I don't like them. They've got long nasty beaks! *And* they wet their nests.
Assistant   But . . . but you can't expect them to produce a special edition for gannet-haters!
Customer   I'm sorry, I specially want the one without the gannet.

The assistant is speechless.

Assistant   All right!

He suddenly tears out the relevant page.

Assistant   Anything else?

Customer Well, I'm not too keen on robins.
Assistant Right! Robins, robins . . .

He tears that one out too and slams the book on the counter.

Assistant No gannets, no robins – there's your book!
Customer I can't buy *that*. It's torn.
Assistant . . . So it is!

He tosses it into the bin.

Customer I wonder if you've got . . .
Assistant Go on! Ask me another.
Customer How about 'Biggles Combs his Hair'?
Assistant No, no, we haven't got that one, funny. Try me again.
Customer 'The Gospel According to Charlie Drake'?
Assistant No . . .
Customer Have you got . . . 'Ethel the Aardvark Goes Quantity-Surveying'?
Assistant No, no, we haven't . . . *which* one?
Customer 'Ethel the Aardvark Goes Quantity-Surveying'.
Assistant 'Ethel the Aardvark'?! I've seen it! We've got it!!

He dashes to a bookshelf, finds it, and holds it up triumphantly.

Assistant Here! Here!!! 'Ethel the Aardvark Goes Quantity-Surveying'. Now – buy it!

He slams it on the desk. The customer stares in horror!

Customer . . . I haven't got enough money on me.
Assistant (*quickly*) I'll take a deposit!
Customer I haven't got *any* money on me.
Assistant I'll take a cheque!
Customer I haven't got a cheque book!
Assistant It's all right, I've got a blank one!
Customer I don't have a bank account!!
Assistant . . . All right!! I'll buy it for you!

He rings the purchase up and pays for it himself. He gives the change to the customer.

There we are, there's your change – that's for the taxi home ...

Customer Wait! Wait! Wait!

Assistant What? What? What?!!!

Customer ... I can't read ...

Assistant Right! Sit!! ...

He sits the customer down on his knees and starts to read aloud.

Assistant 'Ethel the Aardvark was trotting down the lane one lovely summer day, trottety-trottety-trot, when she saw a nice Quantity-Surveyor ...'

(Original cast: Assistant *MV*; Customer *Marty Feldman*)

Arthur 'Two-Sheds' Jackson Skit

by MV and Graham Chapman;
'Monty Python's Flying Circus', 5 October 1969

A standard TV interview set. The interviewer and Jackson are seated in front of a screen on which various images can be projected. At the start, the image is that of a musical score. The introductory music fades.

Interviewer Last week the Royal Festival Hall saw the first performance of a new symphony by one of the world's leading modern composers, Arthur 'Two-Sheds' Jackson. Good evening, Mr Jackson.

Jackson   Good evening.

Interviewer   May I just sidetrack you for one moment, Mr Jackson. This, what shall I call it, nickname of yours . . .

Jackson   Oh yes.

Interviewer   'Two-sheds'.

Jackson   Yes.

Interviewer   How did you come by it?

Jackson   Well I don't use it myself, it's just that a few of my friends call me 'Two-Sheds'.

Interviewer   And do you in fact *have* two sheds?

Jackson   No, I've only got *one* shed – I've had one for some time but a few years ago I said I was thinking of getting another one, and since then some people have called me 'Two Sheds'.

Interviewer   In spite of the fact that you have only one?

Jackson   Yes.

Interviewer   I see. And are you still thinking of purchasing a second shed?

Jackson   No.

Interviewer   To bring you in line with your epithet . . .?

Jackson   No, I'm not.

Interviewer   I see. Well, let's return to your symphony. Did you, in fact, write this symphony *in* the shed?

Jackson   No!

Interviewer   Have you written *any* of your recent works in this shed of yours?

Jackson   No, it's just a *perfectly ordinary* garden shed . . .

On the screen behind them appears the picture of a garden shed.

Interviewer   I see. Were you originally thinking of buying the second shed to write in?

Jackson   No, no – look, this shed business, it doesn't really matter – the sheds aren't important, it's just a few friends call me 'Two-Sheds' and that's all there is to it. I'm a composer. I wish you'd ask me about my music. People are always asking about the sheds. They've got out of proportion. I think I'll get rid of the shed. I wish I'd never got it in the first place.

Interviewer   Then you'd be Arthur 'No-Sheds' Jackson.

Jackson   Look, forget about the sheds, will you? They don't matter.

Interviewer   Ah, Mr Jackson, with respect, I think we ought to talk about your symphony.

Jackson   What?

Interviewer   Apparently your symphony was written for organ and tympani . . .

Jackson catches sight of the picture of the garden shed behind him.

Jackson   What's that?

Interviewer   What's what?

Jackson   It's a shed. Get it off.

He points at the screen. The image of the shed is replaced by a picture of Jackson.

Jackson   Right.

A caption appears under the picture of Jackson reading 'Arthur Two-Sheds Jackson'. Then the image changes to that of two sheds, one with a large question mark over it.

Interviewer   Now Mr Jackson, about your symphony. I understand that you used to be interested in train-spotting.

Jackson   . . . *What?*

Interviewer   I understand that about forty years ago you were quite interested in train-spotting.

Jackson   What's that got to do with my bloody music?

Enter a second interviewer.

Second Interviewer   Are you having any trouble from him?

Interviewer   A little.

Second Interviewer   We interviewers are more than a match for the likes of you, Two-Sheds.

Interviewer (*rising*)   Yes – make yourself scarce, Two-Sheds. This studio isn't big enough for the three of us.

The interviewers grab Jackson and hustle him away.

Jackson   . . . What are you doing?!

Jackson disappears with a crash.

Second Interviewer (*shouting after him*)   Get your own Arts programme, you fairy!

The First Interviewer turns to the camera with a knowing smile.

Interviewer   Arthur 'Two-Sheds' Jackson.

(Original cast: First Interviewer *Eric Idle*; Arthur Jackson *Terry Jones*; Second Interviewer *MV*)

The Last Supper Skit

by MV;
from Amnesty Gala 'A Poke in the Eye with a Sharp Stick', 1, 2 and 3 April 1976

An impressive Papal Person sits on a ritzy throne in the middle of a large Catholic sort of room. We hear a cry of 'Michelangelo to see the Pope'. An attendant enters.

Attendant   Michelangelo to see you, Your Holiness.
Pope   Show him in.

Michelangelo enters.

Michelangelo 'Evening, Your Grace.

Pope Good evening, Michelangelo. I want to have a word with you about this 'Last Supper' of yours.

Michelangelo Oh yes?

Pope I'm not happy with it.

Michelangelo Oh, dear. It took *hours*.

Pope Not happy at all . . .

Michelangelo Do the jellies worry you? No, they add a bit of colour, don't they? Oh, I know – you don't like the kangaroo.

Pope . . . *What* kangaroo?

Michelangelo I'll alter it, no sweat.

Pope I never saw a kangaroo!

Michelangelo Well, it's right at the back, but I'll paint it out, no problem. I'll make it into a disciple.

Pope Ah!

Michelangelo All right now?

Pope That's the problem.

Michelangelo What is?

Pope The disciples.

Michelangelo Are they too Jewish? I made Judas the *most* Jewish.

Pope No, no – it's just that there are twenty-eight of them.

Michelangelo Well, another one would hardly notice, then. So I'll make the kangaroo into a disciple . . .

Pope No!!

Michelangelo . . . All right, all right . . . we'll lose the kangaroo altogether – I don't mind, I was never completely happy with it . . .

Pope That's not the point. There are twenty-eight disciples.

Michelangelo . . . Too many?

Pope Of course it's too many!

Michelangelo Well, in a way, but I wanted to give the impression of a huge get-together . . . you know, a *real* Last Supper – not any old supper, but a proper final *treat* . . . a real mother of a blow-out . . .

Pope There were only twelve disciples at the Last Supper.

Michelangelo . . . Supposing some of the others happened to drop by?

Pope There were only twelve disciples *altogether*.

Michelangelo Well, maybe they'd invited some friends?

Pope   There were only twelve disciples and Our Lord at the Last Supper. The Bible clearly says so.

Michelangelo ... No friends?

Pope   *No* friends.

Michelangelo ... Waiters?

Pope   No!

Michelangelo ... Cabaret?

Pope   No!!

Michelangelo But you see, I *like* them. They fill out the canvas. I mean, I suppose we could lose three or four of them, you know, make them ...

Pope (*loudly, ex cathedra*) There were only twelve disciples and our Lord at the Last ...

Michelangelo I've got it, I've got it!!! We'll call it ... 'The Penultimate Supper'.

Pope   What?

Michelangelo There must have been one. I mean, if there was a last one, there must have been one before that, right?

Pope   Yes, but ...

Michelangelo Right, so this is the 'Penultimate Supper'. The Bible doesn't say how many people were at *that*, does it?

Pope   Er, no, but ...

Michelangelo Well, there you are, then.

Pope   Look!! the Last Supper is a significant event in the life of Our Lord. The Penultimate Supper was *not* ... even if they had a conjurer and a steel band. Now I commissioned a Last Supper from you, and a Last Supper I want!

Michelangelo Yes, but look ...

Pope   With twelve disciples and one Christ!

Michelangelo ... One?!

Pope   Yes, *one*.

Michelangelo is momentarily speechless.

Pope   Now will you please tell me what in God's name possessed you to paint this with *three* Christs in it?

Michelangelo It works, mate!!

Pope   It does *not* work!

Michelangelo   It does, it looks great! The fat one balances the
two skinny ones!

Pope (*brooking no argument*)   There was only *one* Saviour . . .

Michelangelo   I know that, everyone knows *that*, but what about a
bit of artistic licence?

Pope (*bellowing*)   *One Redeemer*!!

Michelangelo (*shouting back*)   I'll tell you what you want, mate . . .
you want a *bloody photographer, not a creative artist with
some imagination*!!

Pope   I'll *tell* you what I want – I want a Last Supper, with one
Christ, twelve disciples, no kangaroos, by Thursday
lunch, or you don't get paid!!

Michelangelo   You bloody fascist!!

Pope   Look, I'm the bloody *Pope* I am! I may not know much
about art, but I know what I like . . .

(Original cast: Michelangelo *Jonathan Lynn*; A Pope
MV)

Merchant Banker Skit

by MV;
'Monty Python's Flying Circus', 9 November 1972

*A very plush office. At a huge desk sits a Merchant Banker.
He is on the telephone.*

Merchant Banker   . . . Yes, I'm glad to say that I've got the
go-ahead to lend you the money you require. We will of
course want as security the deeds of your house, of your
aunt's house, of your second cousin's house, of your
wife's parents' house and of your granny's bungalow;

and we will in addition need a controlling interest in your new company, unrestricted access to your private bank account, the deposit in our vaults of your three children as hostages, and full legal indemnity against any acts of embezzlement carried out against you by any members of our staff during the normal course of their duties . . . No, I'm afraid we couldn't accept your dog instead of your youngest child, but we would like to suggest a brand new scheme of ours under which 51 per cent of both your dog and your wife pass to us in the event of your suffering a serious accident . . . Not at all, nice to do business with you.

He rings off and speaks on the intercom.

Merchant Banker Miss Godfrey, could you send in Mr Ford, please. Now, where's that dictionary?

He opens the dictionary.

Merchant Banker 'Inner life' . . . ah, here we are . . .

But there is a knock at the door.

Merchant Banker Come in!

Enter a little man carrying a tray of charity badges and a collecting tin.

Merchant Banker Ah, Mr Ford, isn't it!
Ford That's right, yes.
Merchant Banker How do you do. I am a Merchant Banker.
Ford How do you do, Mr . . . er . . .?
Merchant Banker Oh! Er . . . I forget my name for the moment, but I *am* a Merchant Banker. Now what can I do for you?
Ford I wondered whether you'd like to contribute to the Orphans' Home.

He rattles the tin.

Merchant Banker   Well, I don't want to show my hand too early, but actually here at Slater-Nazi we are quite keen to get into orphans. You know, developing market and all that . . . what sort of sum did you have in mind?

Ford   Well, you're a rich man . . .

Merchant Banker   Yes, I am. Yes. Yes! Very, very rich. Quite phenomenally wealthy . . . Yes, I do own the most startling quantities of cash, quite right! You're a smart young lad, aren't you? We could do with someone like you to feed the pantomine horse. Very smart.

Ford   Thank you, sir.

Merchant Banker   Now, you were saying – I'm very, very, very, very, very, very, very, very, very, very, very, very rich . . .

Ford   So, um . . . how about a pound?

Merchant Banker   A pound? Yes, I see . . . Now, this loan would be secured by the deposits of . . .

Ford   Er . . . it's not a loan, sir . . .

Merchant Banker   What?

Ford   It's not a loan.

Merchant Banker   Ah.

Ford   You get one of these, sir.

He holds up a paper badge.

Merchant Banker   It's a bit small for a share certificate, isn't it?

He takes it and peers at it.

Merchant Banker   Look, I think I'd better run this over to our legal department. If you could possibly pop back on Friday . . .

Ford   Do you have to do that? I mean . . . couldn't you just give me the pound?

Merchant Banker   Yes, but you see, I don't know what it's *for*.

Ford   It's for the Orphans.

Merchant Banker   Yes?

Ford   It's a gift.

Merchant Banker   . . . A what?

Ford   A gift.

Merchant Banker   Ah, a *gift*! A tax dodge!

Ford   No, no, no . . .

Merchant Banker   No? Well, I'm awfully sorry, I don't understand. Can you just explain exactly what you want?

Ford   Well, I want you to give me a pound, and then I go away and give it to the Orphans.

Merchant Banker   . . . Yes?

Ford   Well, that's it.

Merchant Banker   . . . No, no, I don't follow this at all. Look, I don't want to seem stupid, but . . . it looks to me as though I'm a pound down on the deal.

Ford   Well, yes, you are.

Merchant Banker   I am?! Well, what is my incentive to give you the pound?

Ford   Well, the incentive is to make the Orphans happy.

Merchant Banker   . . . Oh dear. Are you quite sure you've got this right?

Ford   Yes . . . *lots* of people give me money.

Merchant Banker   Just like that?

Ford   Yes.

Merchant Banker   I don't suppose you give me a list of their names and addresses, could you?

Ford   No . . . I just go up to them in the street and ask.

Merchant Banker   Good Lord!!

He rises from his desk.

Merchant Banker   That's the most exciting new idea I've heard in years!! It's so simple it's brilliant!

He takes the tin from Mr Ford.

Well, if that idea of yours isn't worth a pound, I'd like to know what is!

Ford   Oh thank you, sir.

Merchant Banker   The only trouble is, you gave me the idea before I'd given you the pound. And that's not good business.

Ford   Isn't it?

Merchant Banker   No, I'm afraid it isn't. So, um . . . off you go.

> *The Merchant Banker pulls a large lever in the wall. A trapdoor opens in the floor beneath Mr Ford, who duly disappears into it. The Merchant Banker calls after him.*

Nice to do business with you!

(Original cast: Merchant Banker *MV*; Mr Ford *Terence Parry Jones*)

Cricket Commentators Skit

by MV and David Hatch;
'I'm Sorry I'll Read That Again', 3 April 1964

Edward   Welcome to Lord's, and we greet you with the news that the West Indies are 226 for 3 wickets. I'm sorry, the South Africans are 71 for 1. And it's England in the field, and doing jolly well. Don't you think they're doing jolly well, Peter.

Peter   Oh, absolutely first-rate, jolly good indeed. Brian?

Brian   Oh, jolly well indeed, I couldn't agree with you more if I tried. Jolly, jolly good.

Edward   Well, anyway, it's been a thoroughly good morning's cricket so far, don't you think so, Brian?

Brian   Absolutely.

Peter   Oh, jolly good.

Edward   First-rate.

Brian   Very entertaining.

Edward   Absolutely enthralling.

Peter	Jolly absorbing.
Brian	Jolly absorbing.
Peter	Jolly, jolly absorbing.
Edward	It has been rather *slow* so far – in fact, in just over an hour and a half, only three runs have been added. All of them leg-byes. But it has all been jolly absorbing. Jolly absorbing. Don't you think so, Denis?

Pause.

Edward	Oh, he's not here.
Brian	Well, let's see who's batting, then.
Peter	Right, jolly good.
Edward	Ah, now, it's the West In. . . no, it's the South Africans, and the score is . . . now, which one of those is the total?
Peter	I think . . . I think it's the one in the middle.
Edward	Oh yes, that's right. They're 71 for 3. Good heavens – they must have lost another two wickets! Pity we missed that.
Brian	Well, anyway, England now have had a thoroughly good morning in the field.
Edward	You know, Brian, I've got a nasty feeling England are batting.
Brian	Batting? Oh dear, really?
Peter	The batsmen are wearing English caps, aren't they.
Brian	They're not wearing caps at all!
Peter	Oh, no, they're not, are they. I've made one of my mistakes, haven't I? Ha, ha, ha.
Edward	Well, anyway, up here we all think that England are batting. And it must be Peter Godard bowling, don't you think so, Brian?
Brian	I don't know. I just don't know.
Peter	Yes, that's right, absolutely right, it's Trevor Goddard bowling.
Edward	And he's walking back to his mark – he stops, turns, characteristic little skip at the beginning of his run and he's coming in, one, two, three, four, six, seven, eight, five, nine, ten, eleven, thirteen and he bowls . . . and what happened to *that* one, Peter?
Peter	Ah . . . ah . . . I think he got a touch down the leg side.

Brian	Oh, I thought it hit him on the pad.
Edward	Anyway, the ball's gone down the leg side . . . no, wait a moment, he's hit it past cover for four! Beautiful shot! Past cover's left hand.
Brian	No, no – the ball went straight through to the wicket-keeper.
Edward	So it did! So it *did*! He didn't get a touch. Straight through to the wicket-keeper.
Peter	I think he touched it.
Edward	Yes – yes, he was dropped at gully. Put down in the gully! Put down *in* the gully by . . . Grace, I think. A *bad* miss.
Peter	*Bad, bad* miss!
Brian	No, no, no! Wait a moment. He's walking back to the pavilion. I think . . . to change his bat.
Edward	Ah, yes.
Peter	Oh, no, no, no, he's chasing off a dog! Oh, no, wait a minute . . .
Brian	No, wait a minute . . . he's been given out!
Edward	Out!
Peter	Out!
Edward	Out!!
Brian	He's out!!
Peter	He's out!!
Edward	He's out!!
Brian	He's out!!
Peter	He's out!!
Edward	He's *out*!!
Brian	Out!!! Out!!! Out!!! He's . . . *out*!!!!!

Pause.

Edward	. . . *Silly* shot!
Peter	Silly shot.
Brian	Silly silly shot.
Peter	Rash stroke!!
Brian	Rash stroke!!
Peter	Head *right* in the air!!
Edward	So . . . that's England number four, caught at the wicket . . .

Peter	I think he was bowled. Look, the leg stump's missing. See?
Edward	So it is, so it is. Must have been stumped.
Brian	Or run out, trying to sweep.
Peter	No, no, clean bowled. Silly shot.
Brian	Silly shot.

Pause.

Brian	. . . What a silly shot. But we have had a jolly good morning's cricket, haven't we?
Edward	Oh, absolutely.
Brian	Well, that's Cowdrey, bowled Goddard . . . No no, he's *not* out!
Edward	He's *not* out!
Peter	He's not out at all! Well, well!

Pause.

Brian	What a relief for England!
Edward	What a relief.
Peter	What a *relief*!!
Brian	Cowdrey is *still* there with . . . ah . . . anyway, he's still there.
Edward	He's still there.
Peter	So he is.
Brian	And what a good morning's cricket we've had.
Brian	Jolly good.
Edward	Jolly, jolly good. So we return you to the studio with the news that we've all had . . . a *thoroughly* entertaining and absorbing morning's gin and tonic.
Brian	And for me please.
Peter	Make that eight.

(Original cast: Edward *MV*; Peter *Tim Brooke-Taylor*; Brian *David Hatch*)

Fairly Silly Court Skit

by MV and Graham Chapman;
'Monty Python's Flying Circus', 11 October 1969

*A packed courtroom. Everyone is sitting around waiting
patiently. Suddenly there is a noise at the back of the court.
People perk up and turn to observe the Prosecuting Counsel
enter.*

Prosecuting Counsel   I'm sorry I'm late, m'lud – I couldn't find a
kosher car park.

He crosses and takes his proper position.

Don't bother to recap, m'lud, I'll pick it up as we go
along. Call Mrs Fiona Lewis.

Usher   Call Mrs Fiona Lewis!

*Mrs Lewis enters at a considerable speed, talking loudly, and
makes for the witness box.*

Lewis   I swear to tell the truth, the whole truth, and nothing
but the truth, so *anyway* . . . I said to her, I said, they
can't afford that on what he earns, I mean for a start the
feathers get up your nose, I ask you, four and sixpence a
pound, and him with a wooden leg, I don't know how
she puts up with it after all the trouble she's had with
her you-know-what, anyway, it *was* a white wedding,
much to everyone's surprise, of course they bought
everything on the hire purchase, I think they ought to
send them back where they came from, I mean you've
got to be cruel to be kind, so Mrs Harris said, so she
said she said she said, a dead crab she said she said?
Well, her sister's gone to Rhodesia, what with her womb
and all, and her youngest, as fit as a filing cabinet, and
the goldfish, the goldfish, they've got whooping-cough,

they keep spitting water at the Bratbys, well, they *do*, don't they, I mean, you *can't*, can you, I mean they're not even married or anything, they're not even *divorced*, and he's in the KGB if you ask me, he says he's a tree surgeon, but I don't like the sound of his liver, all that squeaking and banging every night till the small hours, well, his mother's been much better since she had her head off . . .

At a sign from the Prosecuting Counsel, two ushers enter and carry Mrs Lewis out, still talking. The judge leans forward.

Judge   Mr Bartlett, I fail to see the relevance of the last witness's testimony.

Prosecuting Counsel My *next* witness will provide an explanation if m'ludship will allow. Call the late Arthur Aldridge.

Usher   Call the late Arthur Aldridge!

A pause.

Judge   The *late* Arthur Aldridge?

Prosecuting Counsel Yes m'lud.

A coffin is carried into the courtroom and laid with some difficulty across the witness box. The judge stares at it.

Judge   Mr Bartlett, is there any point in questioning the deceased?

Prosecuting Counsel I beg your pardon m'lud?

Judge   Well . . . your witness is dead, is he not?

Prosecuting Counsel Yes m'lud. Well . . . *virtually*, m'lud.

Judge   He's not *completely* dead?

Prosecuting Counsel Oh no, he's not completely dead, m'lud. But he's not at all well.

Judge   If he's *not* dead . . . what's he doing in a coffin?

Prosecuting Counsel It's purely a precaution, m'lud. Now, if I may continue . . . Mr Aldridge, you were . . . you *are* a stockbroker of 10, Brian Close, Wimbledon.

A knocking sound is heard.

Prosecuting Counsel   Mr Aldridge, would it . . .

Judge   What was that knock?

Prosecuting Counsel   It means 'yes', m'lud. One knock for 'yes', and two for 'no'. If I may continue . . . Mr Aldridge, would it be fair to say that you are not at all well?

Another knock is heard.

Prosecuting Counsel   In fact, Mr Aldridge, not to put too fine a point on it, would you be prepared to say that you are, as it were, what is generally known as, in a manner of speaking, 'dead'?

Silence.

Prosecuting Counsel   I think he *is* dead, m'lud. Mr Aldridge . . . I put it to you that you are dead.

More silence. The Prosecuting Counsel points accusingly at the coffin.

Prosecuting Counsel   Ah ha!

Judge   Where is all this leading?

Prosecuting Counsel   That will become apparent in a moment, m'lud.

He walks over to the coffin, raises the lid and peers inside for a long time.

Prosecuting Counsel   No further questions, m'lud.

He replaces the lid.

Judge   What do you mean?! You can't just dump dead bodies in my court and say 'No further questions'! I demand an explanation!

Prosecuting Counsel   There are no easy answers in this case, m'lud.

Judge   I think you haven't the slightest idea what this case is about.

Prosecuting Counsel M'lud, the strange, damnable, almost diabolic threads of this extraordinary tangled web of intrigue will shortly, m'lud, reveal a plot so fiendish, so infernal, so heinous . . .

Judge Mr Bartlett, your client has already pleaded guilty to the parking offence.

Prosecuting Counsel Parking offence, schmarking offence, m'lud. We must leave no stone unturned. Call Cardinal Richelieu.

Judge You're just trying to spin this one out, Mr Bartlett.

The judge does a double-take.

Judge *Cardinal Richelieu???*

Prosecuting Counsel A character witness, m'lud.

A fanfare of trumpets. Enter Cardinal Richelieu in full Louis XIII period gear and holding a hand mike, which he handles expertly.

Richelieu 'Allo everyone, it's wonderful to be here y'know. I love your country, London is so beautiful at this time of year.

Prosecuting Counsel You are Cardinal Armand du Plessis de Richelieu, First Minister of Louis XIII?

Richelieu Oui.

Prosecuting Counsel Cardinal, would it be fair to say that you not only built up the centralised monarchy in France but also perpetuated the religious schism in Europe?

Richelieu (*modestly*) That's what they say.

Prosecuting Counsel Did you persecute the Huguenots?

Richelieu I did that thing.

Prosecuting Counsel And did you take even sterner measures against the great Catholic nobles who made common cause with foreign foes in defence of their feudal independence?

Richelieu Certainement!

Prosecuting Counsel Cardinal, are you acquainted with the defendant, Harold Larch?

Richelieu Since I was so 'igh.

Prosecuting Counsel Speaking as a Cardinal of the Roman

Catholic Church, as First Minister of Louis XIII and as one of the architects of the modern world already, would you say that Harold Larch was a man of good character?

Richelieu   Listen – 'Arry is a very wonderful and warm 'uman being.

Prosecuting Counsel   M'lud, in view of the impeccable nature of this character witness, may I plead for clemency.

Judge   It's only thirty shillings.

Enter a Police Inspector at speed.

Inspector Dim   Not so fast!

Prisoner   Why not?

Dim (*momentarily thrown*)   . . . None of your smart answers! You think you're so clever . . . well, *I*'m Dim.

A caption fills the entire screen 'Dim of the Yard!'

All   Consternation! Uproar! Dim!

Dim   Yes, and I've a few questions I'd like to ask Cardinal so-called Richelieu.

Richelieu   Bonjour Monsieur le flic Dim.

Dim   So-called 'Cardinal' . . . I put it to you that you died in December 1642.

Richelieu   That is correct.

Dim   Aha! He fell for my little trap.

Excited applause from the courtroom. Dim bows. Richelieu is dismayed.

Richelieu   Curse you, Inspector Dim, you are too clever for us naughty people.

Dim   Furthermore, I suggest you are none other than Ron Higgins, professional Cardinal Richelieu impersonator.

Richelieu   It's a fair cop.

Prosecuting Counsel   My life, you're clever, Dim. He'd certainly taken us in.

Dim   It's all in a day's work, sir.

Judge   With a brilliant mind like yours, Dim, you could be something other than a policeman.

Dim   True!
Judge   What?

A piano plays an introduction. Dim clears his throat and starts to sing.

Dim   'If I were not in the CID,
          Something else I'd like to be,
          If I were not in the CID,
          A window cleaner, me!
          With a rub-a-dub-dub and a scrub-a-dub-dub
          And a rub-a-dub all day long,
          With a rub-a-dub-dub and a scrub-a-dub-dub
          I'd sing this merry song.'

The court joins in and sings the second verse with him. At the end of the second verse the Prosecuting Counsel rises and sings.

Prosecuting Counsel   'If I was not before the bar
           Something else I'd like to be,
           If I was not a bar-ris-tar.
           An engine-driver, me!
           With a chuff-chuff-chuff . . .'

He suddenly notices that the rest of the court are staring at him in complete amazement. His confidence fades rapidly.

Prosecuting Counsel   . . . chuff . . . chuff . . . chuff?

A knight in armour walks up behind him and hits him over the head with a dead chicken.

(Original cast: Prosecuting Counsel *MV*; Mrs Fiona Lewis *Graham Chapman*; Judge *Terry Jones*; Cardinal Richelieu *Michael Palin*; Inspector Dim *Graham Chapman*)

Crunchy Frog Skit

by MV and Graham Chapman;
'Monty Python's Flying Circus', 23 November 1969

A modern but not particularly smart office. Mr Arthur Hilton sits at his desk, working. The door opens and Inspector Praline and Superintendent Parrot enter.

Praline   Mr Hilton?
Hilton   Yes?
Praline   You are sole proprietor and owner of the Whizzo Chocolate Company?
Hilton   I am.
Praline   Superintendent Parrot and I are from the Hygiene Squad. We want to have a word with you about your box of chocolates entitled the Whizzo Quality Assortment.

He indicates a large box of Whizzo chocolates carried by Superintendent Parrot.

Hilton   Yes?

Inspector Praline opens the box and produces a chocolate.

Praline   To begin at the beginning, first there is the Cherry Fondue. This is extremely nasty. But we can't prosecute you for that.
Hilton   Agreed.

Inspector Praline produces another chocolate and compares it with his notes.

Praline   Next we have number four, Crunchy Frog.
Hilton   Yes.
Praline   Am I right in thinking there's a real frog in here?
Hilton   Yes. A little one.

Praline   What *sort* of frog?

Hilton   A dead frog.

Praline   Is it cooked?

Hilton   No.

Praline   What, a *raw* frog?

Hilton   We use only the finest baby frogs, dew picked and flown from Iraq, cleansed in finest quality spring water, lightly killed and then sealed in a succulent Swiss quintuple smooth full cream treble milk chocolate envelope and lovingly frosted with glucose.

Praline   That's as maybe. It's still a frog.

Hilton   What else?

Praline   Well, don't you even take the bones out?

Hilton   If we took the bones out it wouldn't be Crunchy, would it?

Parrot   Will you excuse me a moment?

Looking a little green, he exits rapidly. Hilton points at the box.

Hilton   It says Crunchy Frog very clearly.

Praline   The general public won't expect a *real* frog in this chocolate – the superintendent thought it was an almond whirl – people are bound to think it's some form of mock frog.

Hilton   *Mock* frog?! We use no artificial flavouring or additives of any kind!

Praline   *Nevertheless* . . . I advise you in future to replace the words Crunchy Frog with the legend Crunchy Raw Unboned Real Dead Frog if you want to avoid prosecution.

Hilton   What about our sales?

Praline   I'm not interested in your sales, I have to protect the public. Now how about this one?

Superintendent Parrot re-enters. Inspector Praline holds up another chocolate and checks his notes.

Praline   It was number five, wasn't it, Superintendent?

Superintendent Parrot nods.

Praline   Number five ... Ram's Bladder Cup.

Superintendent Parrot glares and then exits again at speed.

Praline   What kind of confection is this?
Hilton   We use only choicest juicy chunks of fresh Cornish
                 Ram's bladder, emptied, steamed, flavoured with sesame
                 seeds, slipped into a fondue and garnished with lark's
                 vomit.
Praline   *Lark's vomit!?!*
Hilton   Correct.

Inspector Praline examines the box with alarm.

Praline   It doesn't say anything about lark's vomit here ...
Hilton   It says on the bottom of the box ... there, after
                 monosodium glutamate.

Inspector Praline turns the box over.

Praline   I hardly think this is good enough ... I think it would
                 be *more* appropriate if the box bore a large red label ...
                 'Warning – Lark's Vomit!'
Hilton   Our sales would plummet.
Praline   Well why don't you move into more conventional areas
                 of confectionery? Like Praline and Lime Cream, a very
                 popular flavour I'm led to understand, or Strawberry
                 Delight, I mean look at these ...

*He reads off the lid of the box as Superintendent Parrot
returns.*

Praline   Cockroach Cluster, Phlegm Cream, Anthrax
                 Ripple ...

*Superintendent Parrot exits again making a strange gurgling
noise.*

                 And what's this – Spring Surprise?
Hilton   That's our speciality. When you pop it in your mouth,

steel bolts spring out and plunge straight through both cheeks.

Praline   Well where's the pleasure of that? If people place a nice chocky in their mouth, they don't want their cheeks pierced. In any case this is an inadequate description of the sweetmeat. I shall have to ask you to accompany me to the station.

Hilton rises.

Hilton (*to camera*)   It's a fair cop.
Praline   And don't talk to the camera.

Enter Superintendent Parrot looking pale.

Praline   Ah, Superintendent! Would you say the punch line, please?

Superintendent Parrot turns to the camera and delivers the punch line.

(Original cast: Inspector Praline *MV*; Mr Hilton *Terry Jones*; Superintendent Parrot *Graham Chapman*)

Regella Skit

solo by MV;
'Double Take', Footlights Revue 1962

Good evening. I want to talk to you tonight about the bright star you can see on the eastern horizon at about half-past ten any evening this month. Now this star is called Regella. Re...gel...la. It is at the moment one of the *brightest* stars in the *sky*. In fact, it's just over thirty-five *thousand* times as bright as an ordinary *forty...watt...bulb*!

Now, Regella is also a very *big* star, three hundred and sixty-five *million* miles in diameter, or to put it another way – if you imagine that this *orange*... (*he produces an orange*) ... was as big as the dome of St Paul's Cathedral, then Regella is two hundred and eighty-six *million* times the size of *Waterloo Station*. And to give you some idea of how large two hundred and eighty-six million is – twenty people dotting continuously at a rate of three-and-a-quarter dots a second for four months and three weeks would fill two warehouses with exercise books.

Now, as well as being so *bright* and so *big*, Regella is also a *very* ... *long* ... *way* ... *away* – four hundred and twelve light-years, or the same distance that an *ordinary* white rhinoceros running at an average speed of twenty-two miles per hour would travel if he or she ran for two hundred and eighty-six *million* years; or two-and-a-quarter hundred thousand billion times the width of a budgerigar's wing.

So much for Regella. Next week I shall be showing you how to make what we scientists call a 'lemon meringue pie'.

Hearing-Aid Skit

by MV and Graham Chapman;
'At Last the 1948 Show', 10 October 1967

*A smart modern Opticians shop, which also displays notices
and goods pertaining to the problems of the hard of hearing.
An assistant, Mr Rogers, stands behind the counter
rearranging some hearing aids. A customer enters a little
nervously and approaches him.*

Customer Good morning. I'm interested in buying a hearing
aid.
Rogers ... I'm sorry?
Customer I'm interested in buying a hearing aid.
Rogers ... I didn't *quite* catch it.
Customer (*louder*)   I want to buy a hearing aid.
Rogers ... Hang on a moment, I'll switch the radio off.

*He goes to the radio and switches it on. Loud music issues
forth, making it very hard to hear what is being said.*

Rogers Now, sir, what were you saying?
Customer *What?*
Rogers What were you saying?
Customer I *can't hear* ...
Rogers What?
Customer The *radio's too loud*!
Rogers Yes, it's better now, isn't it.

The customer goes to the radio and switches it off again.

Customer I'm sorry, I couldn't hear what you were saying.
Rogers Pardon? ...

He stares at the customer. A thought strikes him.

Rogers   Oh, wait a moment! I think my hearing aid's switched off.

He pulls out his aid and examines it.

Rogers   Yes, here we are! Excuse me, but I've only had it a few days.

He adjusts it.

Rogers   Yes, that's better – it's on now.
Customer Is it good?
Rogers   About fourteen guineas.
Customer Yes, but is it *good*?
Rogers   No, it fits in the pocket, here.

He demonstrates.

Customer . . . Can you hear me?
Rogers   . . . What?
Customer *Can you hear me?!*
Rogers   . . . Oh, I see! Contact *lenses.*
Customer What?
Rogers   You want contact lenses.
Customer No.
Rogers   I'll get Dr Waring then, because he does the lenses.

He presses a buzzer on the counter.

Rogers   I only do the hearing aids, you see.
Customer Yes, but . . .

Dr Waring appears from an inner office. He stares around, blinking a lot, walks into a door jamb, and then wanders wide-eyed across the shop till he finds himself standing close to the assistant. He addresses him.

Dr Waring   Good morning, sir. You want some lenses, do you?
Rogers   What?

Dr Waring You want some lenses, do you?

Rogers ... I can't quite hear what you're saying, Dr Waring.

Dr Waring I think you need a hearing aid, sir, not lenses! Ha, ha.

Customer No, *I'm* the one who wants the hearing aid.

Dr Waring Who said that? Is there someone else here?

He peers around.

Rogers What?

Dr Waring I think there's somebody else here.

Customer Yes, it's me. Here.

Dr Waring Ah now, you're the gentleman who wanted the contact lenses.

Customer No, I wanted a hearing aid.

Dr Waring Ah well, Mr Rogers will deal with you. (*He shouts.*) Someone to see you, Mr Rogers!! (*To the customer.*) He'll be here in a moment.

He turns to the assistant.

Dr Waring Now *you* wanted the contact lenses, did you, sir? Come this way, please.

Rogers What?

Dr Waring This way ...

He indicates the way. The assistant is puzzled but follows Dr Waring anyway.

Rogers I don't understand.

Dr Waring and Mr Rogers disappear into the inner office. A pause. They reappear, arguing.

Dr Waring Well, why didn't you *say* you were Rogers?

Rogers What?

Dr Waring You know my lenses play me up sometimes.

Dr Waring leaves Rogers and approaches an empty space several feet from the customer. He addresses the space.

Dr Waring   I do apologise for that confusion. Now, you wanted lenses, did you?

Customer Er! . . . I wanted a hearing aid.

Dr Waring (*to the customer*)   Ah, no, Mr Rogers will deal with you, sir. I'll deal with this gentleman. Now, sir, if you'd like to come this way, we'll try some lenses . . . after you.

He indicates the inner office and ushers the empty space into it. A pause.

Customer Excuse me, Mr Rogers . . . (*loudly*) I . . . want . . . a hearing . . . aid.

He touches the assistant's arm.

Rogers   Look, I'm worried about Dr Waring – I think he thinks he's with someone.

We hear Dr Waring shouting in his office.

Dr Waring (*from afar*)   Hallo? Hall-oooo? Hall-oooo?

Customer Well, had you better go and tell him?

Rogers   No, I'd better go and tell him.

He goes to Dr Waring's office, opens the door and calls inside.

Rogers   Dr Waring?

Dr Waring   Ah, *there* you are! I thought I'd lost you.

Rogers   Dr Waring, you're not with anybody.

Dr Waring   Well who's that talking to me? Don't be silly. Sit down.

Rogers   . . . Pardon?

The door is closed. A pause. The door opens and they come out.

Dr Waring   Well, why didn't you *say* you were Rogers?

Rogers   About a quarter past four.

Dr Waring peers round, spots another empty space, and goes to speak to it.

Dr Waring   Are you the gentleman who wanted the contact lenses?
Customer No, *I* wanted the hearing aid!

Dr Waring turns to the customer.

Dr Waring   So *you* must want the contact lenses.
Customer (*screaming*)   *I want a hearing aid!!!*
Dr Waring   Oh! These two gentlemen want hearing aids, Rogers.
Rogers   You know, I don't think my hearing aid's working properly. Hang on.

He takes the aid out and bangs it a couple of times. A horrible high-pitched whine comes from it. Rogers claps his hands to his ears and shakes his head about.

Rogers   Ow! Agh! Help! It's so loud it hurts! Aagh!

He hits the aid again and the whine stops. Rogers heaves a sigh of relief and relaxes.

Rogers   Ah. That's better . . .

He suddenly stares hard and his jaw goes slack.

Rogers   Oh my God – I've knocked my contact lenses out! Don't move!

He drops to the floor and stars feeling around for them. The ~~shop door buzzes open and another customer enters.~~ *He is angry.*

Second Customer (*shouting*)   I want to complain about my contact lenses!   ·

Dr Waring turns to the first customer.

Dr Waring (*surprised*)   What?

The second customer sees a large cut-out of a girl in bikini advertising Kodak films and storms up to it.

Second Customer   I want to complain about my contact lenses.
          They're terrible. They've ruined my eyesight.
Dr Waring (*to the first customer*)   I haven't given you any.
Second Customer   You're a liar!
Dr Waring   What?!
Second Customer   You quack!

> *Dr Waring shakes a finger at the first customer.*

Dr Waring   Don't you speak to me like that!
Second Customer   I'll speak to you how I want.

> *The second customer barks his shins on the startled Rogers.*

          Ow! How *dare* you!
Dr Waring   What?
Second Customer   Rough stuff, eh?
Dr Waring   If that's the way you want it.

> *The first customer backs away.*

Customer   Keep away from me!
Dr Waring   Ah, backing out, now, are you?

> *The second customer treads on the cowering Rogers, takes a
> swing at him and falls through the window. Dr Waring hears
> the crash.*

Dr Waring   Smash my shop up, would you?

> *Rogers, terrified, stands up and brushes against Dr Waring
> who grabs him.*

Dr Waring   Got you!
Rogers   Help! Help! I'm being attacked!!

> *Dr Waring and Rogers grapple furiously.*

Rogers   Help me, Dr Waring!
Dr Waring   It's all right, Rogers, I've got him.

Rogers gets his arms round Dr Waring's waist.

Rogers   I've got him, Dr Waring! Grab his arms.

Dr Waring   I can't, he's got me round the waist! Never mind – let's throw him out!

Rogers   I'm going to throw him out.

Dr Waring   Attack Mr Rogers, would you – we're more than a match for you.

They wrestle each other towards the door. The first customer emerges from hiding to watch.

Rogers   Quick – he's got me round the throat!

Dr Waring   It's all right, I've got him round the throat.

They bump into the door jamb.

Rogers   We're at the door!

Dr Waring   Right – throw him out.

Rogers   One . . .

Rogers and Doctor Waring   Two . . . Threeeeee!

They throw each other out through the door with a tremendous crash. A long pause. Then the first customer, left alone in the shop, turns to the camera, winks and delivers the punch line.

Customer   You should see them when they've had a couple of drinks.

(Original cast: First Customer *Marty Feldman*; Rogers *MV*; Waring *Graham Chapman*; Second Customer *Tim Brooke-Taylor*)

Argument Skit

by MV and Graham Chapman;
'Monty Python's Flying Circus', 2 November 1972

A large, slightly dusty educational type of institution. In the reception area sits a person of the female persuasion, typing. Mr Reg Punter enters and approaches her.

Punter   Good morning.
Receptionist   Good morning, sir. Can I help you?
Punter   Well, I'd like to have an argument, please.
Receptionist   Certainly, sir. Have you been here before?
Punter   No, this is my first time.
Receptionist   I see. Do you want to have a single argument, or were you thinking of taking a course?
Punter   Well . . . what would be the cost?
Receptionist   It's two pounds for a five-minute argument, but only fifteen pounds for a course of ten.
Punter   I see . . . well, I think it's probably best if I start with the one, and see how it goes . . .
Receptionist   Fine – I'll see who's free at the moment.

She consults her file.

Receptionist   Er . . . Mr Ouspensky is free, but he's a little bit conciliatory. Yes . . . try Mr Nicoll, Room 12.
Punter   Thank you.

Punter walks in the direction indicated, sees Room 12, knocks and enters.

Nicoll (*shouting*)   What do you want?
Punter   . . . Well, I was told outside . . .
Nicol   Don't give me that, you snotty-faced heap of parrot droppings!
Punter   What?!
Nicol   Shut your festering gob, you tit! Your type makes me

	puke! You vacuous, toffee-nosed, scrofulous pervert!
Punter	Look! I came in here for an argument, not to be . . .
Nicoll	Oh! . . . Oh, I'm sorry! This is *Abuse.*
Punter	. . . Ah!
Nicoll	No, no. You want 12A, next door.
Punter	I see, sorry!
Nicoll	Not at all, that's all right.

Punter exits.

| Nicoll | Stupid git. |

Punter goes to the next door, and knocks.

| Bennett | Come in! |

Punter enters.

Punter	Er . . . Is this the right room for an argument?
Bennett	. . . I've told you *once.*
Punter	No you haven't.
Bennett	Yes I have.
Punter	When?
Bennett	Just now!
Punter	No you didn't.
Bennett	Yes I did.
Punter	Didn't.
Bennett	Did.
Punter	Didn't
Bennett	I'm telling you I did!
Punter	You did not!
Bennett	Oh, I'm sorry . . . I should have asked . . . Is this a five-minute argument or the full half hour?
Punter	Oh!

He smiles with relief.

| Punter | Just the five-minute one. |

Bennett notes this.

Bennett Fine . . . thank you. Anyway, I did.

Punter You most certainly did not.

Bennett Now let's get one thing *quite* clear. I most definitely told you.

Punter You did not.

Bennett Yes I did.

Punter You did not.

Bennett Yes I did.

Punter You didn't.

Bennett Yes I did.

Punter You didn't.

Bennett Yes I did.

Punter You didn't.

Bennett Yes I did.

Punter Didn't!

Bennett Yes I did.

Punter . . . Look, *this* isn't an argument.

Bennett Yes it is.

Punter No it isn't, it's just contradiction.

Bennett No it isn't!

Punter Yes it is.

Bennett It is not!

Punter It is! You just contradicted me!

Bennett No I didn't!

Punter Ooh, you did!

Bennett No, no, no, no, no . . .

Punter You did, just then!

Bennett Nonsense.

Punter Oh, look . . . this is futile.

Bennett No it isn't!

Punter I came here for a good argument.

Bennett No you didn't. You came here for an *argument*.

Punter Well, argument's not the same as contradiction.

Bennett It can be.

Punter No it can't! An argument's a collected series of statements to establish a definite proposition.

Bennett No it isn't!

Punter Yes it is, it isn't just contradiction.

Bennett Look, if I argue with you, I must take up a contrary position.

Punter   But it isn't just saying 'No it isn't'.
Bennett Yes it is!
Punter   It isn't. Argument's an intellectual process –
             contradiction is just the automatic gainsaying of anything
             the other person says.
Bennett No it isn't.
Punter   Yes it *is*!
Bennett Not at all.
Punter   Now look, I . . .

*Bennett suddenly rings a bell on his desk, notes the time and
makes an entry in a file. Punter stares.*

Bennett Thank you. Good morning.
Punter   What?
Bennett That's it . . . good morning.
Punter   But I was just getting interested.
Bennett Sorry, the five minutes is over.
Punter   . . . That was *never* five minutes . . .
Bennett I'm afraid it was.
Punter (*quickly*)   No it wasn't!
Bennett . . . Sorry. I'm not allowed to argue any more.
Punter   What?
Bennett If you want me to go on arguing, you'll have to pay for
             another five minutes.
Punter   But that was never five minutes just now . . . Oh, come on!

A pause.

Punter   Oh, this is ridiculous!
Bennett I'm very sorry, but as I told you, I'm not allowed to
             argue unless you pay.
Punter   Oh, all right . . .

Punter takes his wallet out and gives Bennett the fee.

Punter   There you are.
Bennett Thank you.

Bennett pockets it and looks at Punter.

Punter Well?

Bennett 'Well' what?

Punter That was never five minutes just now.

Bennett (*with great patience*) I told you, I'm not allowed to argue unless you pay.

Punter (*flabbergasted*) . . . I just paid!

Bennett No you didn't.

Punter I did!

Bennett You didn't!

Punter I did!

Bennett You didn't!

Punter I did! Look – I don't want to argue about that.

Bennett Well, I'm very sorry, but you didn't pay!

Punter . . . Aha! Well, if I didn't pay, why are you arguing?

A pause.

Punter Got you!

Bennett . . . No you haven't.

Punter Yes I have! If you're arguing, I *must* have paid.

Bennett Not necessarily . . . I *could* be arguing in my spare time.

Punter Oh, I've had enough of this.

Bennett (*quickly*) No you haven't!

Punter Oh, shut up!

Punter storms out of the room and walks hurriedly into another skit.

(Original cast: Mr Punter *Michael Palin*; Mr Nicoll *Graham Chapman*; Mr Bennett *MV*)

The Good Old Days Skit

by MV, Marty Feldman, Graham Chapman and
Tim Brooke-Taylor;
'At Last the 1948 Show', 31 October 1967

It is sundowner time at a tropical paradise. Four north-countrymen, in late middle-age and tuxedos, sit contemplating the sunset. A dusky waiter pours some claret for one of them to taste.

Joshua . . . Very passable. Not bad at all.

The waiter pours the wine for the rest of them, and departs.

Obadiah . . . Can't beat a good glass of Château de Chasselas, eh, Josiah?

Josiah Aye, you're right there, Obadiah.

Ezekiel . . . Who'd have thought . . . forty years ago . . . that we'd be sitting here, drinking Château de Chasselas . . .?

Joshua Aye! . . . In those days we were glad to have the price of a cup of tea.

Obadiah Aye, a cup of *cold* tea . . .

Ezekiel Without milk or sugar.

Josiah *Or* tea . . .

Joshua Aye, and a cracked cup at that!

Ezekiel We never had a cup . . . We used to drink out of a rolled-up newspaper.

Obadiah Best we could manage was to chew a piece of damp cloth.

Josiah But y'know . . . we were happier in those days, although we were poor.

Joshua *Because* we were poor . . . My old dad used to say, 'Money doesn't bring you happiness, son.'

Ezekiel He was right! I was happier then and I had *nothing*. We used to live in a tiny old tumbledown house with great holes in the roof.

Obadiah A house! You were lucky to have a house. We used to live in one room, twenty-six of us, no furniture, and half the floor was missing. We were all huddled in one corner, for fear of falling.

Josiah   You were lucky to have a room! We used to live in the corridor.

Joshua   Ooooh! I used to *dream* of living in a corridor. That would have been a palace to us. We lived in an old water tank in the rubbish tip. We were woken up every morning by having a load of rotting fish dumped on us. House, huh!

Ezekiel   Well, when I said *house* . . . it was only a hole in the ground covered by a couple of foot of torn canvas, but it was a house to *us*.

Obadiah   We were evicted from our hole in the ground. We had to go and live in the lake.

Josiah   Eee! You were lucky to have a lake. There were over 150 of us living in a small shoe box in the middle of the road.

Joshua   A *cardboard* box?

Josiah   Yes.

Joshua   You were lucky. We lived for three months in a rolled-up newspaper in a septic tank. We used to get up at six, clean the newspaper, eat a crust of stale bread, work fourteen hours at the mill, day-in, day-out, for sixpence a week, come home, and dad would thrash us to sleep with his belt.

Obadiah   . . . Luxury! We used to get out of the lake at three, clean it, eat a handful of hot gravel, work twenty hours at t'mill for twopence a month, come home, and dad would beat us about the head and neck with a broken bottle, *if* we were *lucky*.

A pause.

Josiah   . . . Aye, well, we had it *tough*. I had to get out of the shoebox at midnight, lick the road clean, eat a couple of bits of cold gravel, work twenty-three hours a day at the mill for a penny every four years and when we got home dad would slice us in half with a bread-knife.

A longer pause.

Ezekiel   Right ... I had to get up in the morning at ten o'clock at night half-an-hour before I went to bed, eat a lump of poison, work twenty-nine hours a day at t'mill and pay boss to let us work, come home, and each night dad used to kill us and dance about on our graves, singing.

A very long pause.

Joshua   ... Aye, and you try and tell the young people of today that, and they won't believe you.

(Original cast: Joshua *Marty Feldman*; Obadiah *Graham Chapman*; Josiah *Tim Brooke-Taylor*; Ezekiel *MV*)

Lucky Gypsy Skit

by MV and Marty Feldman;
'At Last the 1948 Show', 22 February 1967

A street. A street vendor in gypsy uniform is handling clothes-pegs.

Vendor   Clothes-pegs! Genuine gypsy clothes-pegs!

A city gentleman walks by.

Vendor   Clothes-pegs, sir?
City Gent   No, you grotty little man, go away.

The vendor hurries after him.

Vendor   Lucky gypsy clothes-pegs, sir?
City Gent   Go away or I shall call the Army.
Vendor   Thank you, sir! You've got a lucky face, sir.
City Gent   Stop following me!
Vendor   Lucky gypsy clothes-pegs, sir.
City Gent   What do you mean, *lucky* gypsy clothes-pegs? They're probably from Korea.
Vendor   Lucky Korean gypsy clothes-pegs, sir?
City Gent   Go away, you excrementitious, importuning hawker-person.

The city gent walks off. The vendor pursues him and kicks him hard in the bottom. The gent spins round.

City Gent   What are you doing?
Vendor   Lucky gypsy kick, sir! One shilling, sir!
City Gent   What do you mean, one shilling?! I'm not paying you for *kicking* me!!

The vendor pokes him carefully in the eye.

Vendor   Lucky gypsy poke in the eye, sir? Two-and-ninepence? Bring you luck, sir! God bless you, sir.
City Gent   How *dare* you?!

The vendor grabs the city gent's bowler hat and starts dancing about on it.

Vendor   Lucky gypsy trample-on-your-hat, sir? 'Gypsy boot through your hat, nothing luckier than that.' Old saying, sir. Good luck, sir.

He puts his hand out.

Vendor   Five bob sir.
City Gent   Help!

The vendor belts him in the stomach.

Vendor   Lucky gypsy punch in the belly, sir. There you are, sir. Only one pound, can't say fairer than that.

The vendor now hits the city gent in the side of the neck. The latter collapses, stunned.

Vendor   Lucky gypsy karate chop, sir. Only thirty shillings sir, good luck.

He takes the city gent's wallet and kicks him in the ribs.

Vendor   Lucky gypsy robbery with violence, sir.

He opens the wallet.

Vendor   Oh, thank you, sir! You're a real toff, sir. You made an old gypsy very happy, sir. Good luck, sir.

He runs off happily.

Vendor   God bless you, sir! May fortune smile on you, sir!

(Original cast: Vendor *Marty Feldman*; City Gent *MV*)

Mrs Beulah Premise and Mrs Wanda Conclusion visit Mr and Mrs J. P. Sartre Skit

by MV and Graham Chapman;
'Monty Python's Flying Circus', 19 October 1972

A laundromat. Mrs Premise, a pepperpot, sits reading a tabloid. Mrs Conclusion approaches.

Mrs Conclusion Hullo, Mrs Premise.

Mrs Premise Hullo, Mrs Conclusion!

Mrs Conclusion Busy day?

Mrs Premise Busy? I just spent four hours burying the cat.

Mrs Conclusion *Four hours* to bury a cat?

Mrs Premise Yes! It wouldn't keep still, wriggling about howling.

Mrs Conclusion Oh – it wasn't dead, then?

Mrs Premise No, no. But it's not a well cat, so as we were going away for a fortnight's holiday I thought I'd better bury it just to be on the safe side.

Mrs Conclusion Quite right. You don't want to come back from Sorrento to a dead cat. It'd be so anticlimactic. Yes, kill it *now*, that's what I say. We're going to have to have our budgie put down.

Mrs Premise Is it very old?

Mrs Conclusion No, we just don't like it. We're going to take it to the vet tomorrow.

Mrs Premise Tell me, how do they put budgies down, then?

Mrs Conclusion Well, it's funny you should ask that, because I've just been reading a great big book about how to put your budgie down, and apparently, you can either hit them with the book, or you can shoot them just there, just above the beak.

Mrs Premise Just there? Well, well, well. 'Course, Mrs Essence flushed hers down the loo.

Mrs Conclusion   No, you shouldn't do that – no, that's dangerous. They *breed* in the *sewers* and eventually you get evil-smelling flocks of huge soiled budgerigars flying out of people's lavatories infringing their personal freedom.

Mrs Premise   It's a funny thing, freedom. I mean, how can any of us be *really* free . . . while we still have personal possessions.

Mrs Conclusion   You can't! You can't, I mean, how can I go off and join Frelimo when I've got nine more instalments to pay on the fridge?

Mrs Premise   Well, of course, this is the whole crux of Jean-Paul Sartre's *Roads to Freedom*.

Mrs Conclusion   No it isn't! The nub of that is . . . that the characters stand for *all* of *us* in their desire to avoid action. Mind you . . . the man at the off-licence says it's an everyday story of French country folk.

Mrs Premise   What does he know? Sixty new pence for a bottle of Maltese claret. Huh! Well I personally think that Jean-Paul's masterwork is an allegory of man's search for commitment.

Mrs Conclusion   No it isn't.

Mrs Premise   Yes it is!

Mrs Conclusion   'Tisn't.

Mrs Premise   'Tis!

Mrs Conclusion   'Tisn't!

Mrs Premise   All right! We can soon settle this. We'll ask him.

Mrs Conclusion   . . . Do you know him then?

Mrs Premise   Oh yes! We met him on holiday last year.

Mrs Conclusion   In Ibiza?

Mrs Premise   Yes, he was staying there with his wife, and Mr and Mrs Genet. Oh, I did get on well with Madame S.

Mrs Conclusion   What's Jean-Paul like?

Mrs Premise   Well, you know . . . bit moody. Didn't join in the fun much. Just sat there thinking. Still, Mr Rotter caught him a few times with the whoopee cushion. Oooh, we *did* laugh!!

Mrs Conclusion   Well let's give him a tinkle, then.

Mrs Premise   All right. She said they were in the book.

> *Mrs Premise calls out to the other denizens of the laundromat.*

Mrs Premise   Where's the Paris telephone directory?
Mrs Inference   It's on the drier.

> *Mrs Premise goes to the drier and sees several telephone directories.*

Mrs Premise   Budapest . . . Pyong Yang . . . here we are! Sartre . . . Sartre . . .
Mrs Proposition   It's 612036.
Mrs Premise   Oh, thank you, Mrs Proposition.

> *Mrs Premise dials. As they wait for the number to connect, they sing 'The Girl from Ipanema'.*

Mrs Premise   . . . Hallo? Hallo, Mrs Sartre! It's Beulah Premise here. Oh! C'est Beulah Premise ici. Oui, oui, dans Ibiza. Oui. We met . . . nous nous rencontrons en Hôtel Miramar. Oui, à la Barbecue, Madame S. Est-ce que Jean-Paul est chez vous? Oh merde. When will he be free? Oh – er . . . pardon . . . quand sera-t'il libre? Oooooh! Ha ha ha. (*To Mrs Conclusion.*) She says he's spent the last sixty years trying to work that one out! (*To Madame Sartre.*) Très amusant, Madame S. . . Absolument. A bientôt.

> *Mrs Premise rings off.*

Mrs Premise   Well, he's out distributing pamphlets to the masses but he'll be in at six.
Mrs Conclusion   I'll ring BEA then.

> *A Parisian street thronged with typical Frenchmen with loaves, berets and bicycles. Mrs Premise and Mrs Conclusion approach an apartment block and peer at the list of tenants.*

Mrs Premise   Here we are, number 25!
Mrs Conclusion   Flat 1 – Duke and Duchess of Windsor. Flat 2,

Yves Montand. Flat 3, Jacques Cousteau. Flat 4, Jean Genet and friend. Flat 5, Maurice Leroux . . .

Mrs Premise   Who's he?

Mrs Conclusion   Never heard of him. Flat 6, Marcel Marceau 'Walking Against the Wind Ltd'. Flat 7, Indira Gandhi . . .

Mrs Premise   She gets about a bit, doesn't she?

Mrs Conclusion   Flat 8, Jean-Paul and Betty-Muriel Sartre!

Mrs Conclusion rings the appropriate buzzer.

Intercom Voice   Oui?

Mrs Premise   C'est nous, Betty-Muriel.

Intercom Voice   Entrez!

The buzzer sounds.

Mrs Premise   Merci!

They enter the block, and go to the Sartres' flat. The door is opened by Madame Sartre, a rat-bag with a fag in her mouth and a duster over her hair.

Madame Sartre   Bonjour!

Mrs Conclusion   Er . . . parlez-vous anglais?

Madame Sartre   Yes. Good day!

She sees Beulah Premise.

Hallo, love!

Mrs Premise   Hullo! This is Mrs Conclusion from no. 46.

Madame Sartre   Nice to meet you, dear.

They enter the Sartre's apartment.

Mrs Premise   How's the old man?

Madame Sartre   Don't ask. He's in one of his bleedin' moods. 'The bourgeoisie this – the bourgeoisie that . . .' He's like a little child sometimes. I was only telling the Rainiers the other day – 'course he's always rude to

them, the only classy friends we've got – 'Solidarity with
the masses', I said. 'Pie in the sky!' Oooh! . . . You're
not a Marxist, are you, Mrs Conclusion?

Mrs Conclusion No, I'm a Revisionist.

Madame Sartre Oh good. I mean, look at this place! I'm at my
wit's end. Revolutionary leaflets everywhere. One of
these days I'll revolutionary leaflets *him.* You can hardly
put your feet up for propaganda.

Mrs Premise Can we pop in and see him?

Madame Sartre Yes, come along. But be careful. He's had a few.
Mind you, he's as good as gold in the morning, I've got
to hand it to him. But come lunchtime it's six glasses of
vin not-so-ordinaire and he's ready to agitate.

They knock on the door of Jean-Paul's den.

Mrs Premise Oooooooo – Jean-Paul? It's only *us.* Pardon! C'est
nous-mêmes.

The door is opened. They pop their heads inside.

Mrs Premise Jean-Paul, your famous trilogy *Rues à Liberté* . . . is
it an allegory of man's search for commitment?

Sartre Oui.

Mrs Premise (*to Mrs Conclusion*) I told you so.

She shuts the door.

Mrs Premise Well, that's settled then.

(Original cast: Mrs Conclusion *Graham Chapman*; Mrs
Premise *MV*; Mrs Proposition *Michael Palin*; Madame
Sartre *Michael Palin*)

Undertakers Skit

by MV and Graham Chapman;
'Monty Python's Flying Circus', 22 December 1970

*An Undertaker's Emporium. A customer, Mr Bereaved, is
standing by the counter. He rings a bell on the counter, and
an undertaker appears from the back of the shop.*

Undertaker Morning!

Bereaved . . . Good morning.

Undertaker What can I do for you, squire?

Bereaved . . . Well . . . er . . . I wonder if you can help me? . . .
You see . . . my mother's just . . . died.

Undertaker Oh yeah, we can help. We deal with stiffs.

Bereaved . . . What?

Undertaker Now, there are three things we can do with your late
mummy. We can burn her, bury her or dump her.

Bereaved . . . Dump her?

Undertaker Dump her in the Thames . . .

Bereaved What?!

Undertaker Oh! Did you like her?

Bereaved Yes.

Undertaker Ah, well we won't dump her, then. Well, what do
you think? We can bury her, or burn her.

Bereaved Well . . . which do you recommend?

Undertaker They're both nasty . . . If we burn her, she gets
stuffed in the flames, crackle crackle crackle, which is a
bit of a shock if she's not quite dead, but *quick*; then we
give you a handful of ashes which you can pretend are
hers.

Bereaved . . . I see.

Undertaker Or if we *bury* her, she gets eaten up by lots of
weevils and nasty maggots, which, as I said before, is a
bit of a shock if she's not dead.

Bereaved Well, she's definitely dead.

Undertaker Where is she?

Bereaved She's in this sack.

Mr Bereaved reveals a large sack by his feet.

Undertaker Let's have a look.

The undertaker opens the neck of the sack and peers around inside.

Undertaker Oh! She looks quite young.
Bereaved Yes, she was.
Undertaker (*calling*)   Fred!

Another undertaker look round the door at the back of the shop.

Undertaker I think we've got an eater.
Bereaved What?
Second Undertaker I'll put the oven on.
Undertaker Right.

The second undertaker disappears.

Bereaved . . . Excuse me.
Undertaker Yeah?
Bereaved . . . Are you suggesting . . . *eating* . . . my *mother?*
Undertaker Yeah . . .

The undertaker notices the expression on Bereaved's face.

Undertaker Not *raw! Cooked!* Roasted . . . French fries, broccoli . . . horseradish sauce?

A long pause as Bereaved takes this in.

Bereaved (*grudgingly*)   . . . Well, I do feel a bit peckish.
Undertaker (*calling*)   One forty-nine, Fred!
Bereaved Can we have some parsnips?
Undertaker 'Course. (*He calls.*) And a sixteen! (*To Mr Bereaved.*) Right! Now . . . how about stuffing?

Bereaved No, look! Wait a moment . . .

Undertaker . . . What's the matter, squire?

Bereaved Well . . . I don't . . . I'm sorry but I really don't think
we should *eat* her.

Undertaker (*reasurringly*) Look, tell you what . . . we'll eat her.
Then . . . if you feel guilty about it afterwards, we'll dig a
grave and you can throw up in it.

(Original cast: Mr Bereaved *MV*; Undertaker *Graham
Chapman*; Second Undertaker *Eric Idle*)

Railway Carriage Skit

by MV, Graham Chapman and Marty Feldman;
'At Last the 1948 Show', 31 October 1967

*An old-fashioned railway compartment. It is empty, except for
. . . city gent, who sits in a corner by the window, reading*
The Times. *After a few moments, an Annoying Little Man
enters the compartment. He is called Mr Raymond Pest. He
stares at the city gent, and then walks slowly round the
compartment, examining each vacant seat in turn. None of
them meets with his satisfaction. Finally he examines the seat
right next to the city gentleman, poking it with his forefinger.
Then he clears his throat. The city gent looks up.*

City Gent Yes?

Pest   Is this seat occupied?

City Gent No.

Mr Pest sits down next to the city gent, perhaps a little too close for comfort. The city gent studiously ignores him. After a moment, Mr Pest starts fidgeting. He is clearly not comfortable. He tries various different sitting positions, clicking his tongue to indicate his dissatisfaction. The city gent studiously ignores him.

Pest   Excuse me, would you mind chánging seats?
City Gent . . . What?

Mr Pest points at the city gent's seat.

Pest   Can I sit there?
City Gent . . . Very well.

City gent rises and sits in the opposite corner seat. Mr Pest jumps into the vacated seat eagerly. But very soon he is uncomfortable again.

Pest   Hmmmmm . . . hmmmmmmmmmm . . .tch, tch, tch.
City Gent Yes?
Pest   I thought I'd like sitting here. But now that I'm here it's not as good as I thought it would be.
City Gent Oh.

He goes back to reading The Times. *Mr Pest nips across the compartment and sits next to him.*

Pest   Do you mind if I smoke?
City Gent No, not at all.
Pest   . . . You're sure?
City Gent Yes, thank you.

He turns to another page of his paper.

Pest   You're not just saying that to be polite?
City Gent No. Please do smoke.
Pest   . . . You would say if you didn't want me to.
City Gent . . . Yes, I would.
Pest   *Really?*

The city gent gives Mr Pest a long piercing look.

City Gent Yes, I promise I would.
Pest Good. So you don't mind if I smoke?
City Gent No.
Pest Only some people object.
City Gent . . . Yes, but *not* me.

A pause.

Pest I thought I'd just make sure . . .
City Gent Yes, thank you.
Pest You're welcome!
City Gent Thank you.
Pest Not at all . . . It's *my* pleasure.
City Gent . . . Quite.
Pest No effort to ask.
City Gent No . . .
Pest No effort at all.
City Gent Right.
Pest Politeness costs nothing.
City Gent Thank . . . you
Pest Not at all! . . . Thank *you*.
City Gent Not at all.
Pest Thank you though . . .

City gent puts his paper down.

City Gent Look. Go ahead and *smoke* . . .
Pest Thank you.

City gent picks his paper up and starts reading. Mr Pest sits very still. After a time the city gent becomes aware that Mr Pest has not lit a cigarette.

City Gent . . . Why aren't you smoking?
Pest I haven't got a cigarette.
City Gent . . . Do you *want* a cigarette?
Pest Ooooooh!

The city gent puts his paper down and takes out a packet of cigarettes and offers Mr Pest one.

Pest   . . . No, I don't think I should.
City Gent (*steelily*)   Please take one.
Pest   No I oughtn't.
City Gent Take one!
Pest   No really.
City Gent All right.

He puts the cigarettes away and picks his newspaper up again. A pause.

Pest   . . . I wish I hadn't refused that a cigarette.

The city gent slams his newspaper down and gets the cigarettes out again.

Pest   Thank you!

Mr Pest takes a cigarette. The city gent, with great deliberation, takes out a lighter. Mr Pest, however, puts the cigarette in his pocket.

City Gent . . . Aren't you going to smoke it?
Pest   *Oh no!* . . . It's a two-hour journey, and if I smoke it now I won't have one for *after*.
City Gent . . . After what?
Pest   After I've smoked *this* one. If I had *two* cigarettes, it would be plain sailing. Yes! Two cigarettes is what I really need.
City Gent Have another one.

He offers Mr Pest another cigarette. Mr Pest takes it eagerly and the city gent lights it for him. Then he puts his lighter away, picks up his copy of The Times *and determinedly starts reading again.*

Pest   . . . Thank you.
City Gent Not at all.

Pest   No, but thank you anyway.
City Gent Shut up!!

*There is a long pause as the city gent starts to read again, and
Mr Pest puffs contentedly. Suddenly Mr Pest screams. The
city gent jumps.*

City Gent What was that?!
Pest   It was *me*. It's a speech impediment.
City Gent A *speech* impediment?
Pest   Yes. I used to do that after every second word. I used to
say 'Hallo there (*he screams*) Mr Cook (*he screams*). How
are (*he screams*) you this (*he screams*) lovely summer (*he
screams*) morning? *I'm* (*he screams*) fine'.
City Gent Yes, yes, yes, I understand. Now, *please* . . .

*He picks up his newspaper and fixes his attention on it. A
pause.*

Pest   They cured me at the hospital though . . . they were
wonderful . . . they stopped me going (*he screams*) after
every second word . . . Wonderful they were.

City gent cannot concentrate on his reading.

City Gent How did they stop you?
Pest   Well, it's very interesting. They said to me 'Don't go (*he
screams*) after every second word', and it worked! Now I
only go (*he screams*) when I want to.

*City gent is not happy about this answer but picks his paper
up nevertheless. He starts reading. Mr Pest screams very
loudly and the city gent jumps.*

Pest   I wanted to do it then.

*City gent buries himself in his paper, determined not to be
distracted again. Mr Pest starts talking happily.*

Pest   Once upon a time there was a fairy prince called

        Raymond Pest who got on a train and was given
        cigarettes by a wizard. A very clever wizard. *Magic*
        cigarettes.

City Gent What are you *talking* about?!

Pest   I was telling myself a story to pass the time.

City Gent Well, could you please tell it silently then.

*Mr Pest starts telling the story silently. He gesticulates, mimes
the words and plays a number of different characters.
However, the city gent manages to keep his attention on the
paper.*

Pest (*loudly*)   I spy with my little eye something beginning with B
         ... *or* J.

City Gent Quiet!

Pest (*quietly*)   ... It's easy.

City Gent Shut up!

A pause.

Pest   B ... or ... J?

City Gent ... *How* can it begin with a B or a J?

Pest   For various reasons which become apparent when you
      know the answer.

City Gent ... What's the answer?

Pest   Ectoplasm!

City Gent (*astounded*)   Ectoplasm!?!?!?!?

Pest   Yes. Mr B. J. Ectoplasm.

The city gent stares at him slack-jawed.

Pest   He works at our office.

City Gent ... What? *But* ... I can't *see* him!

Pest   You can if you have an appointment.

The city gent glazes over.

Pest   I can disappear.

Silence.

Pest   *I . . . can* disappear!
City Gent . . . Why don't you then?

> *Mr Pest takes a deep breath and disappears.*

City Gent Thank God for that.

> (Original cast: City Gent *MV*; Mr Pest *Marty Feldman*)

Cheese Shop Skit

by MV and Graham Chapman;
'Monty Python's Flying Circus', 30 November 1972

> *A Cheese Emporium. Despite its considerable size, it is quaint
> in an old-fashioned and charming way. An assistant stands
> behind the counter. At the far end of the shop two grey-suited*
> ~~men are doing a Greek dance to the accompaniment of a~~
> *bouzouki. A customer enters.*

Assistant Good morning, sir.
Customer Good morning. I was sitting in the public library in
             Thurmond Street just now, skimming through *Rogue
             Herries* by Horace Walpole, when I suddenly came over
             . . . all esurient.
Assistant Esurient, sir?
Customer Peckish . . .
Assistant . . . Ah!
Customer So I thought to myself, a little fermented curd will do

the trick. Igitur, I curtailed my Walpolling activities, sallied forth, and infiltrated your place of purveyance to negotiate the vending of some cheesy comestibles.

Assistant . . . Come again?

Customer I want to buy some cheese.

Assistant Oh. I thought you were complaining about the music.

Customer Heaven forbid! I am one who delights in all manifestations of the terpsichorean muse.

Assistant Sorry?

Customer I like a nice dance, you're forced to! So my good man . . . some cheese, please . . .

Assistant Yes, certainly, sir. What would you like?

Customer Well, how about a little Red Leicester?

Assistant I'm afraid we're fresh out of Red Leicester, sir.

Customer Never mind. How are you on Tilsit?

Assistant Never at the end of the week, sir, we always get it fresh first thing on Monday.

Customer Tush, tush. No matter. Well, four ounces of Caerphilly, if you please, stout yeoman.

Assistant Ah . . . It's been on order for two weeks. I was expecting it this morning.

Customer I see. It's not my lucky day, is it? Um . . . Bel Paese?

Assistant Sorry, sir.

Customer Red Windsor?

Assistant Normally, sir, yes. But today the van broke down.

Customer Do you have any Stilton?

Assistant Not as such.

Customer Emmenthal?

Assistant We just sold the last slice, sir.

Customer Any Norwegian Jarlsberger?

Assistant I'm afraid not.

Customer Liptauer?

The assistant checks.

Assistant . . . No.

Customer Lancashire?

Assistant . . . No.

Customer White Stilton?

Assistant No.

Customer Danish Blue?
Assistant No.
Customer Double Gloucester?
Assistant No.
Customer Cheshire?
Assistant No.
Customer Any Dorset Blue Vinney?

The assistant checks very carefully.

Assistant . . . No.
Customer Brie? Rocquefort? Pont L'Eveque? Port Salut? Savoyard? Saint Paulin? Carre de L'Est? Boursin? Bresse Bleu? Camembert?
Assistant Ah! We *do* have Camembert, sir.
Customer You do?! Excellent!
Assistant . . . It's a bit *runny*, sir.
Customer Oh, I *like* it runny.
Assistant As a matter of fact, it's *very* runny, sir.
Customer No matter, no matter. Hand over le fromage de la belle France qui s'appelle Camembert, s'il vous plaît.
Assistant . . . I think it's runnier than you'll like, sir.
Customer I don't care how fucking runny it is, my man. Hand it over with all speed.
Assistant Yes sir.

He disappears below the counter to get it. A pause.

Assistant *(out of vision)* Ooohh
Customer What?

The assistant straightens up, looking crestfallen.

Assistant The cat's eaten it.
Customer . . . *Has* he . . .
Assistant *She*, sir.
Customer *(showing grace under pressure)* Gouda?
Assistant No.
Customer Edam?
Assistant No.

Customer Caithness?
Assistant No.
Customer Smoked Austrian?
Assistant No.
Customer Sage Derby?
Assistant No, sir.

A pause. The customer surveys the shop.

Customer You *do* have some cheese, do you?
Assistant Certainly, sir. It's a cheese *shop*, sir. We've got . . .
Customer No, don't tell me! I'm keen to guess . . .
Assistant Fair enough . . .
Customer Wensleydale?
Assistant Yes, sir?
Customer Splendid! Well, I'll have some of that, please.
Assistant Oh, I'm sorry sir! I thought you were referring to me –
Mr Arthur Wensleydale.

A minimal pause.

Customer Gorgonzola?
Assistant Er . . . um . . . n. . .n. . .nope.
Customer Parmesan? Mozzarella? Pippo Crème? Danish Finbo?
Czechoslovakian sheep's milk cheese? . . . Any
Venezuelan Beaver cheese?
Assistant Not *today*, sir.
Customer Well let's keep it simple. How about . . . *Cheddar?*
Assistant I'm afraid we don't get much call for it round these
parts, sir.
Customer *Not much call* for it?! It's the single most popular cheese
in the *world* . . .
Assistant *Not* round these parts, sir.
Customer Pray, what *is* the most popular cheese round these parts,
Mr Wensleydale?
Assistant *Ilchester*, sir.
Customer . . . I see.
Assistant Yes, sir! It's staggeringly popular in this manor, squire.
Customer *Is* it?
Assistant In fact . . . it's our number one seller!

Customer *Is* it now?
Assistant *Yes*, sir!
Customer Ilchester, eh?

> *He digests this information.*

Customer OK, I'm game! 'Have you got any?' he asked, expecting the answer 'No'.
Assistant I'll have a look, sir.

> *Slowly the assistant looks round the shop. This takes some time.*

Assistant Nnnnnn. . .nnn. . nnn. . .o.
Customer (*reflectively*)   . . . It's not much of a cheese shop, is it, really?
Assistant Finest in the district, sir.
Customer And *what* leads you to that conclusion?
Assistant Well, it's so clean, sir!
Customer It's certainly uncontaminated by cheese.
Assistant You haven't asked me about Limberger, sir.
Customer . . . Is it *worth* it?
Assistant Could be . . .
Customer . . . OK! Have you . . .

> *He suddenly spins round and screams at the Greek dancers.*

Customer WILL YOU SHUT THAT BLOODY DANCING UP!!!

> *The dancers stop.*

Assistant (*to the Dancers*)   Told you so . . .

> *The customer clears his throat, straightens his tie, and smiles charmingly.*

Customer Have you got any Limberger?
Assistant (*sadly*)   Nope.
Customer Well, that figures. It was quite predictable really, I

suppose. In fact, it was an act of the purest optimism to have posed the query in the first place. Tell me something . . .

Assistant Yes, sir?

Customer And I want you to answer this question absolutely truthfully . . .

Assistant Very well, sir.

Customer Do you, in fact, have *any* cheese at all?

Assistant No, sir.

The customer pulls out a Colt 45 and shoots the assistant between the eyes.

Customer What a senseless act of violence. Nethertheless, I shall plead contributory negligence.

(Original cast: Assistant *Michael Palin*; Customer *MV*; Dancers *Graham Chapman and Terry Jones*)

String Skit

By MV and Graham Chapman;
'The Frost Report on Advertising', 27 April 1967

A Typical Sprousy Advertising Agency Office. Adrian Wapcaplet sits behind his desk. The client, Mr Simpson, enters and Wapcaplet rises to greet him.

Wapcaplet Ah! Come in, Mr Simpson. Welcome to Follicle, Ampersand, Goosecreature, Eskimo, Sedlitz, Wapcatlet, Looseliver, Vendetta, Wallaby and Spong, London's leading advertising agency. Do sit down. My name's Wapcatlet, Adrian Wapcatlet.

Simpson   How do you do.

They both sit.

Wapcaplet   Now, Mr Simpson – I understand you want us to advertise your washing powder?

Simpson   *String.*

Wapcaplet   String, washing powder – what's the difference! We can sell anything.

Simpson   Good. Well, I have this large quantity of string – 112,000 miles of it to be exact – which I inherited. And I thought that if I advertised it . . .

Wapcaplet   Of course, a national campaign ! Useful stuff, string, no trouble there.

Simpson   Ah, but there's a *snag*, you see. Due to bad planning . . . the 12,000 miles is in 3-inch lengths.

He gives Wapcaplet a sample three-inch length of string.

Simpson   So it's not very useful . . .

Wapcaplet   Three-inch lengths, eh? . . . That's our selling point! Simpson's *individual* Stringettes!

Simpson   . . . What?

Wapcaplet   The 'Now' string . . . pre-sliced, easy-to-handle Simpson's Individual Emperor Stringettes. *Just* the right length!

Simpson   For what?

Wapcaplet   Er . . . a million household uses!

Simpson   Such as?

Wapcaplet   Tying up very small parcels, attaching notes to pigeons' legs, destroying household pests . . .

Simpson   Destroying household pests? How?

Wapcaplet   If they're bigger than a mouse you can strangle them with the string, and if they're smaller you can flog 'em to death with it.

Simpson   But surely . . .

Wapcaplet   Destroy 99 per cent of known household pests with Simpson's pre-sliced rustproof easy-to-handle low-

calorie Individual Emperor Stringettes! Free from
artificial colouring. As used in hospitals.

Simpson Hospitals???

Wapcaplet You ever been in a hospital where they didn't have
string? Buy Simpson's miracle stringettes *today*!

Simpson Miracle? It's only *string*!

Wapcaplet *Only* string? It's everything! It's waterproof!

Simpson No it isn't.

Wapcaplet All right – it's water-resistant, then.

Simpson It isn't.

Wapcaplet ... All right! It's water-*absorbent*! It's ...
*super*absorbent string. Absorb water today with
Simpson's Individual Water Absorbitex Stringettes. Away
with floods!

Simpson You just said it was waterproof ...

Wapcaplet Away with the dull drudgery of workaday tidal waves!
Use Simpson's Individual Space-age Flood Preventers!

Simpson You're mad.

Wapcaplet Shut up, shut up.

*Wapcaplet rises from his desk and paces the office in a creative
frenzy.*

Wapcaplet Now, sex ... sex, we must get sex into it ... Wait! I
see a television commercial ... There's this nude
woman in a bath, holding a bit of your string. That's
great!! But we need a doctor. Got to have a medical
opinion. There's a nude woman in a bath with a doctor.
That's *too* sexy. Put an Archbishop there watching them
– that'll take the curse off it. Now we need children and
animals. There's two kids admiring the string and a dog
admiring the Archbishop, who's blessing the string.
International flavour is missing. Make the Archbishop
Greek Orthodox – why not Archbishop Makarios? No,
he's dead. Never mind – we'll get his brother, it'll be
cheaper. So there's Archbishop Makarios's brother and a
doctor in the bath with this nude woman and two kids
and a dog – no, make that a tiger, that's more
international – and Makarios's brother smiles sexily and
says, 'Prevent household flood today with Simpson's

Individual Stringettes, the International Passport to knot-tying pleasure – destroys 99 per cent of known household pests!

He strikes a triumphant pose. Then a look of disappointment crosses his face.

Wapcaplet   Oh, no, hang on, we can't do that. That's the new Tory Party campaign.

(Original cast: Wapcaplet *Ronnie Barker*, Simpson *Ronnie Corbett*)

Chapel Skit

by MV and Graham Chapman;
'Monty Python's The Meaning of Life', 1983

A School Chapel. Hundreds of intelligent, impressionable young teenagers sit patiently awaiting the end of the service. The senior master is reading the lesson.

Senior Master   And spotteth twice they the camels before the third hour. And so the Midianites went forth to Ram Gilead in Kadesh Bilgemath by Shor Ethra Regalion, to the house of Gash-Bil-Bethuel-Bazola, he who brought the butter dish to Balshazar and the tent peg to the house of Rashomon, and there slew . . . they the goats yea and placed they the bits in little pots. Here endeth the lesson.

The Senior Master closes the bible. The Headmaster rises.

Headmaster   Let us praise God.

The Congregation rises.

Headmaster   Oh Lord . . .
Congregation   Oh Lord . . .
Headmaster   Oooooh, you are *so* big.
Congregation   Oooooh, you are *so big* . . .
Headmaster   So absolutely huge.
Congregation   So ab-sol-utely huge . . .
Headmaster   Gosh, we are all really impressed down here, I can tell you.
Congregation   You can say that again.
Headmaster   I mean, you're so tough and strong, you could beat anybody up.
Congregation   *Especially* the Devil.

A Castrato chants.

Castrato   You would smash his face in . . .
Headmaster   And forgive us, Oh Lord, for this our dreadful toadying . . .
Congregation   And barefaced flattery.
Headmaster   But we are most incredibly impressed 'cos you are *so* strong and . . . well, just so *super.*
Congregation   Fan-tas-tic.

The congregation sits.

Headmaster   Amen. Now two boys have been found rubbing linseed oil into the school cormorant. Now I know some of you feel that the school cormorant does not play an important part in the life of the school, but I would remind you . . . that it was presented to the school by the corporation of the town of Sudbury to commemorate Empire Day, when we try to remember the names of all those from the Sudbury area who so gallantly gave their lives to keep China British. Hymn 42! 'Oh Lord, please don't burn us'.

The organ starts playing and the congregation rises and sings.

Congregation   Oh Lord, please don't burn us,
Don't grill or toast your flock
Don't put us on the barbecue,
Or simmer us in stock
Don't braise or bake or boil us,
Or stir-fry us in a wok.

Oh please don't lightly poach us,
Or baste us with hot fat,
Don't fricassé or roast us,
Or boil us in a vat,
And please don't stick your followers, Lord,
In a Rotissomat.

They all leave the chapel feeling spiritually refreshed.

Original cast:
Senior Master *MV*
Headmaster *Michael Palin*

'Ones' Skit

by MV; from Amnesty Gala
'The Mermaid Frolics', 1977

A Fashionable Knightsbridge Restaurant. It is dinner time. At a romantically lit table sit an upper-class pair, Simon and Fiona, deep in conversation.

Simon	. . . One went to Cruft's, and *guess* who one saw?
Fiona	Who?
Simon	Buffy.
Fiona	One is *so* pleased to see one's old chums again, isn't one?
Simon	Had one heard?
Fiona	What?
Simon	He won a prize!
Fiona	No! Fancy one of one's old chums winning one!
Simon	Yes, one wonders if one's ever known one win one.
Fiona	. . . Pardon?
Simon	One said . . . one wonders when one's known one win one.
Fiona	. . . But one's won one once *oneself*.
Simon	One's won one once oneself?! Darling, how clever of one!
Fiona	No, not one. *One*.

Fiona indicates Simon.

Simon	Oh, *one*! Oh yes, *one's* won one, yes. But one thought one had said one had won one.
Fiona	No darling, *one*.
Simon	But surely . . . when one's said one's won one, one means *oneself* doesn't one . . . not that someone *other* than oneself has won one.
Fiona	No, when one wants, one can mean not one oneself but . . . um . . . another geezer.

Simon   ... Pardon?

Fiona   Sorry darling! Someone other than the one one means, when one means one *other* than one oneself.

Simon   ... Oh, one sees!

Fiona   One's so glad.

Simon takes Fiona's hand tenderly.

Simon   When one's with one's darling ... one feels one's ... one.

Fiona   One won *what*?

Simon   No. One's *at* one ...

Fiona   Oh! At one with *oneself.*

Simon   Not at one with ... *one.*

Fiona smiles.

Fiona   One so agrees.

Simon looks deeply into Fiona's eyes.

Simon   ... One loves one, darling.

Fiona   One loves one too.

She kisses his hand.

Simon   ... Where was one darling?

Fiona   One was saying one's wife didn't understand one ...

(Original cast: Simon *MV*; Fiona *Connie Booth*)

Army Protection Racket Skit

by MV and Michael Palin;
'Monty Python's Flying Circus', 7 December 1969

*The C.O.'s Office at an Army camp. At a desk sits a
distinguished-looking Colonel. There is a knock at the
door.*

Colonel   Come in!

A Sergeant enters.

Sergeant   Two civilian gentlemen to see you, *sir*!
Colonel   Show them in, please, sergeant.
Sergeant   Mr Dino Vercotti and Mr Luigi Vercotti, *sir*!

*Enter the Vercotti Brothers. They are a slightly seedy pair of
gangsters, wearing black shirts, silver ties, dark glasses and
cigarette ash. The sergeant leaves.*

Dino   Good morning, Colonel.
Colonel   Good morning, gentlemen. What can I do for you?
Luigi   . . . You've got a *nice* Army base here, Colonel.
Colonel   Yes.
Luigi   Well . . . we wouldn't want anything to happen to
it.

A pause.

Colonel   . . . What?
Dino   What my brother means is, it would be a shame
if . . .

He knocks an ashtray off the desk. It smashes.

Dino   Oh . . . *sorry*, Colonel.

Colonel	Oh don't worry about it. Do please sit down.
Luigi	No, we prefer to stand, thank you Colonel.
Colonel	Very well. Now, what do you want?
Dino	What do we *want*? Ha, ha, ha. Ha, ha, ha.

They both chortle humourlessly.

Luigi	Ha, ha, very good, Colonel.
Dino	The Colonel's a joker, Luigi!
Luigi	Explain it to the Colonel, Dino.

Dino leans on the desk with his face very close to the Colonel's.

Dino	How many tanks have you got, Colonel?
Colonel	About 500.
Dino	500!

Luigi comes very close to the Colonel on the other side.

Luigi	You ought to be *careful*, Colonel . . . 'Cos things *break*, don't they.
Colonel	. . . Break?
Dino	Well, everything breaks, don't it, Colonel.

Dino knocks a cup and saucer off the desk. They shatter.

Dino	Oh *dear*!
Luigi	You see, my brother's clumsy, Colonel. When he gets unhappy he *breaks* things. Like . . . say he don't feel the Army's playing fair by him, he may start breaking things, Colonel.
Colonel	. . . Look, what *is* all this about?
Luigi	How many men have you got here, Colonel?
Colonel	7,000 Infantry, 600 Artillery, and two divisions of paratroopers.
Luigi	Oooh! Paratroopers, Dino!
Dino	It'd be a shame if someone set fire to *them* . . .
Colonel	. . . *Set fire* to them?!
Luigi	Fires *happen*, Colonel.

Dino comes really close to the Colonel and speaks very quietly.

Dino   My brother and I have got a little proposition for you, Colonel.

Luigi   Would save you a lot of bother . . .

Dino   I mean. You're doing all right, here, aren't you, Colonel?

Luigi   But suppose some of your tanks was to get broken . . . and troops started getting lost . . . and fights started breaking out during General Inspection . . .

Dino   It wouldn't be good for business, would it, Colonel?

Colonel   . . . Are you . . . *threatening* me?

Dino   No, no, no!

Luigi   We're your buddies, Colonel.

Dino   We want to look after you.

Luigi   We can guarantee . . . not a *single* armoured division will get done over, for fifteen bob a week.

Colonel (*decisively*)   No, no, no.

Luigi   Twelve and six a week?

Colonel   No.

Dino   Eight and six . . .

Colonel   No, this is silly.

Dino   . . . What's silly?

Colonel   No, the whole sketch is silly, the premise is weak and it's very badly written. I'm the Senior Officer here and I haven't had a funny line yet. So I'm stopping it.

Dino   . . . You can't do that!

Colonel   I've done it. The sketch is over. Right! *Director* . . . Close *up*! Zoom in on me.

The camera closes in on the Colonel.

Colonel   That's better.

Out of shot, Dino and Luigi complain.

Dino   It's only 'cos he couldn't think of a punch line.

Colonel   Not true, not true. It's time for a cartoon. Cue telecine – ten, nine, eight . . .

Luigi   The general public's not going to understand this, Dino.
Colonel   Shut up, you Eyeties. Three, two, one ...

(Original cast: Colonel *Graham Chapman*; Sergeant *MV*;
Dino Vercotti *Terry Jones*; Luigi Vercotti *Michael Palin*)

Slightly Less Silly than the Other Court Skit Court Skit

(*Aka 'Judge Not'*)
by MV; 'Cambridge Circus', Footlights Revue 1963

A packed Courtroom. The usher enters and addresses those present.

Usher   Be upstanding in Court!

Everyone rises as the judge enters and sits.

Usher   Be downsitting! Call the accused!

Another usher in the bowels of the court takes up the cry.

Second Usher   Call the accused! Call the accused!

Enter Arnold Fitch, the accused, uncertainly.

Clerk of the Court   You are Arnold Fitch?
Fitch   D-d-definitely, yes.

Clerk of the Court   You are hereby accused that on the
fourteenth day of July in the nineteen hundred and
sixty-third year of Our Lord you did wilfully, unlawfully,
and with malice aforethought assault one Sidney Bottle,
a dwarf. How plead you, guilty, or not guilty?

Fitch   D-d-definitely, not guilty.

Mr Bartlett, the Prosecuting Counsel, rises.

Bartlett   M'lud, in this case m'learned friend Mr Maltravers
appears for the defence, and I appear for the money.
The case would appear to be a simple one, m'lud. The
prosecution will endeavour to prove that the snivelling,
depraved, cowardly wretch whom you see cowering
before you . . .

Fitch looks around with curiosity.

Bartlett   . . . returned home on the night of the fourteenth of July
in a particularly vicious and unpleasant frame of mind,
had words with his wife, and then deliberately assaulted
his pet ostrich by throwing a watering can at it.

Judge   A what?

Bartlett   A watering can, m'lud – a large cylindrical tin-plated
vessel with a perforated pouring piece, much used by the
lower classes for the purpose of artificially moistening
the surface soil.

Judge   Thank you, Mr Bartlett.

Bartlett   You are very gracious, m'lud. If I may continue . . . the
ostrich, taking fright . . .

Judge   The what?

Bartlett   The ostrich, m'lud. An ostrich – a large hairy flightless
bird resident in Africa, remarkable for its speed in
running and much prized for its feathers.

Judge   Ah, a kind of kookaburra.

Bartlett   No, m'lud. The ostrich, taking fright, flew through a
window and landed on a passing ice-cream cart . . .

Judge   A *what* cart?

Bartlett   An ice-cream cart, m'lud. Ice-cream – an artificial
cream substitute, sweetened, flavoured and frozen,

originally invented by the Mohican Indians as an
antidote to trench-foot.

Judge   Remarkable, remarkable . . .

Bartlett   Thank you, m'lud; if I may be *allowed* to continue . . .
landed on a passing ice-cream cart, thereby causing a
dollop of ice-cream . . .

Judge   A what?

Bartlett (*screaming*)   A DOLLOP!!!

Consternation in court.

Bartlett   I beg your pardon, m'lud, I'm afraid I was trying to clear
my throat . . . thereby causing a small . . . er, *portion* of
ice-cream to fall on the plaintiff, Mr Sidney Bottle, a
dwarf, who was hopping past at the time, thereby soiling
Mr Bottle's new suit. Those, quite simply, are the facts
of the case, m'lud, a very straightforward one, I think we
will all agree. It would appear m'lud that the rule laid
down in 'Pritchard *v.* the East Halifax Fishbone Glue
Manufacturing Company' would apply.

Judge   Was that the case of the slug in the cherryade bottle, Mr
Bartlett?

Bartlett   No, m'lud, it was the case of the human cannonball and
defective net.

Judge   Ah, *that* was the kookaburra case.

Bartlett   *No*, m'lud.

The Defence Counsel rises

Defence Counsel   I think his Lordship is thinking of 'White *v.*
Phillips' where the Aborigine who was about to launch
his boomerang at a dingo that was chasing his pet
kangaroo, had his attention distracted by a lunging
kookaburra, causing him accidentally to release the
boomerang, which struck a passing cobber in the
outback. An Australian case, m'lud.

Judge   Ah, well, if it was an Australian case, then it cannot
apply.

Defence Counsel   No, m'lud.

Bartlett   *Exactly*, m'lud. If we could continue ... I should like to call the first witness. Call Percy Molar!

The second usher calls in the distance.

Second Usher   Call Percy Molar! Call Percy Molar!

Mr Percy Molar enters at speed. He is dressed as a traditional music-hall comedian.

Molar   'Ello, 'ello, 'ello!
Bartlett   ... Are you Percy Molar?
Molar   That is correct, *that* is correct!
Bartlett   You are a company director of no fixed abode?
Molar   I am.
Bartlett   You are also a music-hall comedian?
Molar   Yes, yes, yes!
Bartlett   Are you marrried?
Molar   Yes, I am, yes I am, my wife!
Bartlett   Would you in your own words please, Mr Molar, describe your wife to this court.
Molar   *My* wife, my *wife* ... she's *so* fat, she's *so* fat ... when she walks down the street she looks like five dogs fighting in a sack! My wife, five dogs, in a sack, thank you!
Bartlett   Thank you, Mr Molar. Would I be correct in thinking that your wife has, comparatively recently, visited the West Indies?
Molar   Yes!
Bartlett   ... Jamaica?

The Defence Counsel leaps to his feet.

Defence Counsel   Objection!
Bartlett   I'm sorry, m'lud! I withdraw that question. Mr Molar ... did you meet your wife in a revolving door?
Molar   No, she went *of her own accord*! I thank you!
Bartlett   No! Now listen very carefully to the question please, Mr Molar ... did you meet your wife in a *revolving* door?

Molar   Ah yes, and we've been going *around together* ever since!

Bartlett   Mr Molar, I put it to you . . . that your mother-in-law is
               bald.

Molar   I agree.

Bartlett   Now would I be correct in assuming . . .

The Defence Counsel is on his feet again.

Defence Counsel   Objection! I hope m'learned friend is not going
               to lead.

Bartlett   I am not . . . Mr Molar, does your mother-in-law . . .

Defence Counsel   Objection!

Bartlett   Did your mother-in-law . . .

Defence Counsel   Objection!

Bartlett   M'lud, I must protest! M'learned friend is making a
               mockery of this Courtroom. What is more, m'learned
               friend is neither learned nor m'friend, and in future,
               with your permission, m'lud, I shall refer to him as
               m'ignorant enemy. And now, if m'ignorant enemy will
               allow me to get a few words in edgeways . . .

Judge   *What* ways, Mr Bartlett?

Bartlett   It's time you retired, m'lud.

The judge consults his pocket watch.

Bartlett   Mr Molar . . . what has happened to your *bald* mother-
               in-law recently?

Molar   She's had rabbits – *rabbits* – tattooed on her head, so
               that at a distance they'll look like *hares*!

Bartlett   Thank you, Mr Molar.

Molar   Bunny-rabbits . . . H. . .a. . .i. . .

Bartlett   Thank you, Mr Molar . . . and did you then see the
               ostrich fly out of the window and land upon a passing
               ice-cream cart, thereby causing a small dollop of ice-
               cream to fall on the plaintiff, Mr Sidney Bottle, a dwarf,
               who was hopping past at the time?

Molar   Yes!

Bartlett   No further questions, m'lud.

He sits. The Defence Counsel rises, studying his notes.

Defence Counsel Just two questions, m'lud. Mr Molar . . .

Molar 'Ello, 'ello, 'ello . . .

Defence Counsel Does your house have a garden?

Molar No, no, my house does definitely not have a garden, my house, not a garden, *no*!

Defence Counsel Do you see the accused?

Molar Yes, yes, yes, yes, yes, yes, yes, yes, yes!

Defence Counsel Does *his* house have a garden?

Molar No, no, the accused, his house does not have a garden, no, no.

Defence Counsel In that case, would the accused be likely to have . . . a spade?

Molar No.

Defence Counsel A scythe?

Molar No.

Defence Counsel A rake?

Molar No.

Defence Counsel Trowel?

Molar No.

Defence Counsel Pitchfork?

Molar No.

Defence Counsel Pruning shears?

Molar No.

Defence Counsel Watering-can?

Molar Yes!

Defence Counsel Damn, damn, damn. No further questions, m'lud.

Judge You may leave the Court, Mr Molar.

Molar You're very kind, m'lud, but before I go I should like to sing a very very lovely Old English Ballad entitty-i-tittled 'She was only a Farmer's Daughter, but . . .'

Judge I don't wish to know that, would you kindly leave the Court.

Molar (*crestfallen*) Very well, m'lud.

He leaves the Courtroom. The Prosecuting Counsel stands again.

Bartlett Call Arnold Fitch.

From afar, the Second Usher calls very loudly and very echoingly.

Second Usher   Call Arnold Fitch! Call Arnold Fitch!

Arnold Fitch makes his way into the witness box.

Bartlett   You are Arnold Fitch, alias . . .

The Second Usher calls again.

Second Usher   Call Arnold Fitch!

A pause as the echoes die away.

Bartlett   You are Arnold Fitch, alias . . .

The usher calls yet again.

Second Usher   Call Arnold Fitch!

A longer pause.

Bartlett   You . . .

Another weird, echoing cry comes from the Second Usher.

Second Usher   Call

The Prosecuting Counsel leaves the Courtroom.

Arn. . .old. . .Fff. . .it. . .

The usher's cry ends in a dreadful gurgle. The Prosecuting Counsel re-enters, wiping his hands with a handkerchief and addresses the witness.

Bartlett   You are Arnold Fitch, alias Arnold Fitch?
Fitch   Yes.

Bartlett   . . . Why is your alias the *same* as your real name?

Fitch   Because, when I use my alias, no one would *expect* it to be my real name.

Bartlett   I see. You are a company director?

Fitch   Of course.

Bartlett   Did you throw the watering can?

Fitch   No.

Bartlett   I suggest that you threw the watering can.

Fitch   I did not.

Bartlett   I put it to you that you threw the watering can.

Fitch   I didn't!

Bartlett   I submit that you threw the watering can!

Fitch   No!

Bartlett   Did you or did you not throw the watering can?!

Fitch   I did not!

Bartlett   *Yes* or *no*?! *Did* you throw the watering can?!

Fitch   No!

Bartlett   *Answer* the question!!!

Fitch   I didn't throw it!

Bartlett   So . . . he *denies* it! . . . Very well . . . would you be surprised to hear that you'd thrown the watering can?

A pause.

Fitch   . . . Yes.

Bartlett   And do you deny *not* throwing the watering can?

Fitch   Yes.

Bartlett (*triumphantly*)   Ha!!!

Fitch   No!!!

Bartlett   Very well, Mr Fitch . . . would it be true to say that you were lying . . . if you denied that it was false to affirm that it belied you to *deny* that it was *untrue* that you were *lying?*!

Fitch   Er . . .

Bartlett   You hesitate, Mr Fitch! An answer, please, the court is waiting! Ah ha ha hah! Ah ha ha hah!

Fitch   Yes.

Bartlett   *Shit.* No further questions, m'lud.

Defence Counsel   Call Exhibit 'A'!

An astonishingly old usher totters in to the court. He is so senile, he may even be older than the judge. He dodders into the well of the court and takes about twenty minutes to set up an old-fashioned baby's bath on a stand. After an aeon, he totters out again.

Defence Counsel   Mr Fitch. Have you ever seen this before?

Fitch   No.

Defence Counsel   No further questions, m'lud.

The Defence Counsel sits, and the palaeozoic usher collects the bath interminably, and eventually exits with it. The accused suddenly has an idea.

Fitch   No, wait a minute!

A dismayed pause. The usher re-enters, at a slightly increased pace, enraged by the extra effort required. He sets the bath up again.

Defence Counsel (*impatient*):   Mr Fitch, I repeat . . . Have you ever seen this before?

Fitch (*brightly*)   Yes, he brought it in a moment ago.

Sensation. Uproar in court. Somehow the bath is removed again. The Prosecuting Counsel rises.

Bartlett   Call Sidney Bottle! . . . Just once!

Second Usher (*from the distance, with difficulty*)   Call Sidney Bottle . . . just once.

There is a long pause. No one appears in the witness box. The Prosecuting Counsel studies his notes, and then addresses the witness box, despite the lack of habitation.

Bartlett   You are Sidney Bottle. You are presumably a company director. You are also a dwarf. Now would you tell the court in your own words what happened on the night of the fourteenth of July.

The Prosecuting Counsel observes that there is no one in the witness box. He looks round the court in puzzlement.

Bartlett (*calling*) Mr Bottle? Mr Bottle!?

Suddenly a tiny hand appears over the top of the witness box and waves frantically. The Prosecuting Counsel points.

Bartlett Ah, there he is, m'lud. Could we give Mr Bottle something to stand on, m'lud, for the benefit of the jury?

Judge Yes, yes, of course.

The decrepit usher appears and enters the box. After a lot of noise, a tiny fist grasps the top of the witness box, followed by another. Eventually Mr Bottle's eyes come into view. He seems remarkably cheerful.

Bartlett Ah. Now, Mr Bottle . . .

But Mr Bottle falls out of sight. He clambers back into view, with difficulty.

Bartlett There you are, Mr Bottle. How nice to see you. Now would you tell the Court please, in your own words of course, on the night in question . . . just exactly how *drunk* were you?!

Bottle Eh?

Bartlett Come come, Mr Bottle, you are not going to pretend that you were sober? I have here a sworn statement, Mr Bottle, that on the night in question you had consumed no less than one hundred and seventeen pink gins!

Bottle starts protesting loudly. The Prosecuting Counsel attempts to continue but the general noise level builds as Mr Bottle becomes more enraged. The judge beckons into the wings, and a dwarf policeman whose helmet and truncheon alone we see, enters the witness box and belabours Mr Bottle. The noise and confusion build to a phoney climax which the

*judge signals when he flings over the edge of his bench a large
sign declaring:* LUNCH.

(Original cast: Clerk of the Court *Bill Oddie*; Arnold
Fitch *Anthony Buffery*; Prosecuting Counsel (Mr Bartlett)
MV; Judge *David Hatch*; Defending Counsel *Chris
Stuart-Clark*; Second usher *Bill Oddie*; Percy Molar *Tim
Brooke-Taylor*; Geriatric usher *Tim Brooke-Taylor*; Sidney
Bottle (a dwarf) *Bill Oddie*)

Courier Skit

Solo by MV (and Graham Chapman);
'The Frost Report on Holidays', 17 March 1966

*A large Courier, in cap and livery, stands at the front of a
motor coach and addresses the passengers.*

Sit down . . . *Sit* down, 18! *Sit*!! *SIT*!! . . . That's your
last warning, 18, next time I strap you in. My God, eight
hours in the coach and you're hysterical . . . what are
you going to be like in *three days*? Pull yourself together,
man, you've only seen five capitals. You've got another
eighteen to go. Right! . . . Wake up, 12, wake *up*!! Now
then . . . in twenty minutes we will be leaving Italy and
entering Switzerland, which is a *different country*. So
finish your spaghetti, throw the cans out of the window,
and put the Primus stoves back under your seats. You

may now open your souvenir plastic bags marked 'Not to be opened till Italy'. You'll find a small green plastic replica of the Tower of Pisa . . . don't try and stand it up, it's *made* that way. Right, now in half a minute we'll be crossing the border. You don't need your passports yet, we've got a special arrangement, they just stamp the coach. We're in Switzerland . . . *now*! Switzerland is famous for its mountains, cheese, clocks and chocolate. Nothing else. Open your plastic bags marked 'Switzerland'. You'll find a small piece of chocolate . . . eat it up quickly, we're not here long, it's a small country. Wake up, 12, *wake up*, there's another capital coming up in a moment . . . I've warned you all before – if you miss a capital you do the whole tour again. Now, Berne, B-E-R-N-E, Berne . . . is coming up on the right-hand side of the coach any moment. Sorry it's getting a bit dark – shine your torches out of the window . . . There it is, over there! Right, tick Berne. Now, Berne is the sixth largest . . . you *missed* that, didn't you, 9? What do you mean, 'you can't find your chocolate' . . . *no* excuses, you've missed a capital! Right, number 9, Thompson, you'll do the whole tour again . . . Stop screaming . . . *Stop* screaming! *Stop* . . . never mind, he's fainted. All right, we'll have an emergency stop here.

There is a squeal of brakes and the coach lurches wildly.

We've stopped. Everyone out! Out, out, out, out, out, out, out, out, out, in, in, in in, *in*, *in*, *in*, *IN*!! . . . You were last, 22, you'll wash the coach. Right, we're off again. Next, the midnight bathe in the crystal clear waters of the Swiss lake as advertised in the brochure . . . the coach will be passing *through* the lake in thirty seconds. So get your swimming costumes on now, open the doors, driver, this is where I leave you, there's another courier waiting for you on the other side of the lake, breathe in when I say 'Breathe in' . . . Breathe in! Good luck, good-bye and *no* drowning.

He leaps expertly from the hurtling coach.

Ethel the Frog Skit

by MV and Graham Chapman;
'Monty Python's Flying Circus', 15 September 1970
A TV Documentary

A Current Affairs Set. A presenter sits at a desk. Stirring music plays. The title of the programme, Ethel the Frog, *is superimposed. The music fades. The presenter looks into camera.*

Presenter   Good evening. On *Ethel the Frog* tonight we look at violence. The violence of British gangland. Last Tuesday a reign of terror was ended when the notorious Piranha brothers, Doug and Dinsdale, were sentenced to over 40,000 years' imprisonment. Tonight, *Ethel the Frog* examines the rise to power of the Piranhas, the methods they used to subjugate rival gangs, and their subsequent tracking down and capture by the brilliant Superintendent Harry 'Snapper' Organs of Q Division. Doug and Dinsdale Piranha were born, on probation, in a house in Kipling Road, Southwark, the eldest sons in a family of sixteen. Their father, Arthur Piranha, a scrap metal dealer and TV quizmaster, was well known to the police, and a devout Catholic. In January 1928 he had married Kitty Malone, an up-and-coming East End boxer. Doug was born in February 1929 and Dinsdale two weeks later; and again a week after that. Their next-door neighbour was Mrs May Simnel.

A South London Street. Mrs Simnel speaks to an interviewer.

Mrs Simnel   Oh, yes. Kipling Road was a typical South London street. People were in and out of each other's houses with each other's property all day.

Interviewer   Was it a very violent neighbourhood?

Mrs Simnel   Ho, ho, yes, cheerful and violent. I remember Doug was very keen on boxing until he learned to walk. Then he took up putting the boot in the groin. Oh, he was very interested in that. His mother had a terrible job getting him to come in for tea. He'd be out there, putting his little boot in, bless him. But you know, kids were very different then – they didn't have their heads filled with all this Cartesian dualism.

In the Studio.

Presenter When the Piranhas left school, they were called up, but were found by an Army board to be too mentally unstable even for National Service. Denied the opportunity to use their talents in the service of their country, they began to operate what they called 'The Operation'. They would select a victim and then threaten to beat him up if he paid them the so-called protection money. Four months later they started another operation which they called 'The Other Operation'. In this racket they selected a victim and threatened not to beat him up if he didn't pay them. One month later they hit upon 'The Other Other Operation'. In this the victim was threatened that if he didn't pay them they would beat him up. This, for the Piranha brothers, was the turning point.

Another South London Street. Superintendent Harry 'Snapper' Organs addresses the camera.

Superintendent Organs Doug and Dinsdale Piranha now formed a gang which they called 'The Gang' and used terror to take over night clubs, billiard halls, gaming casinos and race-tracks. When they tried to take over the MCC they were, for the only time in their lives, slit up a treat. As their empire spread, however, we in 'Q' Division were keeping tabs on their every movement by reading the colour supplements.

In the Studio.

Presenter A small-time operator who fell foul of Dinsdale Piranha was Vince Snetterton-Lewis.

A grotty living-room. Vince Snetterton-Lewis lounges uneasily on a greasy sofa.

Snetterton-Lewis Well, one day I was sitting at home threatening the kids, and I looked out of the hole in the wall, and I saw this tank drive up and one of Dinsdale's boys gets out and he comes up all nice and friendly like, and says Dinsdale wants to have a talk with me, so he chains me to the back of the tank and takes me for a scrape round to Dinsdale's place, and Dinsdale's there in the conversation pit with Doug and Charles Paisley the baby crusher, and a couple of film producers, and a man they called 'Kierkegaard' who just sat there biting the heads off whippets, and Dinsdale just says 'I hear you've been a naughty boy, Clement' and he splits me nostrils open and saws me leg off and pulls me liver out and I said 'My name's *not* Clement'. So he loses his temper and nails my head to the floor.

Interviewer (*in hushed voice*) He nailed your head to the floor?

Snetterton-Lewis At first, yeah.

In the Studio.

Presenter Another man who had his head nailed to the floor was Stig O'Tracy.

A really nasty lounge. Stig O'Tracy slumps on an even greaser sofa.

Interviewer Stig, I've been told that Dinsdale Piranha nailed your head to the floor.

O'Tracy No, no, never! Never. He was a smashing bloke. He used to buy his mother flowers and that. He was like a brother to me.

Interviewer But the police have film of Dinsdale actually nailing your head to the floor.

O'Tracy Oh . . . yeah, well, he did that, yeah.

Interviewer Why?

O'Tracy Well, he *had* to, didn't he? I mean, be fair, there was nothing else he *could* do. I mean, I had transgressed the unwritten law.

Interviewer   What had you done?

O'Tracy   Er . . . well, he never told me that. But he gave me his word that it was the case and that's good enough for me with old Dinsy. I mean, he didn't want to nail my head to the floor. I had to insist. He wanted to let me off. There's nothing Dinsdale wouldn't do for you.

Interviewer   And you don't bear him any grudge?

O'Tracy   A grudge?! Old Dinsy? He was a real darling.

Interviewer   I understand he also nailed your wife's head to a coffee table. Isn't that true, Mrs O'Tracy?

Mrs O'Tracy is sitting in an armchair. She has a coffee table nailed to her head.

O'Tracy   No. Well . . . he *did* do that, yeah. He was a cruel man – but fair.

Vince Snetterton-Lewis's living-room.

Interviewer   Vince, after he nailed your head to the floor, did you ever see him again?

Snetterton-Lewis   Oh yeah. After that, I used to go round to his flat every Sunday lunchtime to apologise, and we'd shake hands. Then he'd nail me head to the floor.

Interviewer   Every Sunday?

Snetterton-Lewis   Yeah. Mind you, he was very reasonable about it. I mean, one Sunday when my parents were coming round for tea, I asked him if he'd mind very much not nailing my head to the floor that week, and he agreed and just screwed my pelvis to a cake-stand

Another really nasty flat. Sid Flange is balancing on a kitchen chair. He has a standard lamp through his lower back and a table lighter stapled to his neck.

Flange   He was the only friend I ever had.

A riverside parking lot. A large block of concrete with a pair of legs sticking out of it. From the block comes a voice.

Voice   I wouldn't hear a word against him.

A gravestone.
It reads 'RIP and Good Luck to Dinsdale'.

In the Studio.

Presenter   Clearly Dinsdale inspired tremendous loyalty and terror amongst his business associates. But what was he really like?

A drinking club. April Strong, a tall woman with rather broad shoulders and a lot of make-up, addresses the camera.

April Strong   I walked out with Dinsdale on many occasions and found him a charming and erudite companion. He was wont to introduce one to many eminent persons, celebrated American singers, members of the aristocracy and other gangleaders.

Interviewer   How had he met them?

April Strong   Through his work for charity. He took a warm interest in Boy's Clubs, Sailor's Homes, Choristers Associations, Scouting Jamborees and of course the Household Cavalry.

Interviewer   Was there anything unusual about him?

April Strong   I should say not. Dinsdale was a perfectly normal person in every way. Except . . . inasmuch as he was convinced that he was being watched by a giant hedgehog whom he referred to as 'Spiny Norman'.

Interviewer   How big was Norman supposed to be?

April Strong   Normally he was wont to be about twelve feet from snout to tail. But when Dinsdale was very depressed, Norman could be anything up to eight hundred yards long. When Norman was about, Dinsdale would go very quiet and his nose would swell up and his teeth would start moving about and he'd become very violent and claim that he'd laid Stanley Baldwin.

Interviewer   Did it worry you that he, for example, stitched people's legs together?

April Strong   It's better than bottling it up, isn't it? He was a gentleman, Dinsdale, and what's more he knew how to treat a female impersonator.

A booklined Study. Dr Hardy-Ling addresses the camera. He looks rather depressed. The words 'A Criminologist' are superimposed.

Hardy-Ling   It is easy for us to judge Dinsdale Piranha too harshly. After all, he only did what most of us simply dream of doing. After all, a murderer is only an extroverted suicide. Dinsdale was a looney, but he was a happy looney . . . lucky bastard.

In the Studio.

Presenter   Most of these strange tales concern Dinsdale, but what of Doug? One man who met him was Luigi Vercotti.

A very tacky office. Luigi Vercotti sits at a grubby desk, below nude girl calendars, and addresses the camera.

Vercotti   I had been running a successful escort agency, no, *really*, high-class girls . . . we didn't have any of that. *That* was right out.

The phone on his desk rings.

Vercotti   Excuse me.

He answers it.

Vercotti   Hallo . . . not now . . . stummm, stummm . . . right, yes we'll have the *watch* ready for you at midnight . . . the watch . . . the *Chinese watch* . . . yes, right . . . 'bye bye . . . mother.

He replaces the phone.

Vercotti   So I decided to open a high-class night club for the gentry at Biggleswade with an international cuisine, cooking and top-line acts, and *not* a cheap clip joint for picking up tarts, that was *right* out, I deny that completely. One night, Dinsdale walked in with a couple of big lads, one of whom was carrying a tactical nuclear missile. They said I had bought one of their fruit machines, and would I pay for it.

Interviewer   How much did they ask?

Vercotti   Three-quarters of a million pounds. Then they left.

Interviewer   ... Why didn't you call for the police?

Vercotti   I'd noticed that the lad with the thermo-nuclear device was the Chief Constable for the area. Anyway, a week later they called again and said the cheque had bounced and said ... I had to see ... Doug.

Interviewer   *Doug.*

Vercotti   Yeah, Doug ... I was terrified of him ... Everyone was terrified of Doug. I've seen grown men pull their own heads off rather than go to see Doug. Even *Dinsdale* was frightened of Doug.

Interviewer   What did Doug do?

Vercotti   He used sarcasm.

In the Studio.

Presenter   By a combination of violence and sarcasm the Piranha brothers by February 1966 controlled London and the South-East. In February, though, Dinsdale made a big

mistake.

Back at the drinking club, April Strong addresses the camera.

April Strong   Latterly Dinsdale had become increasingly worried about Spiny Norman. He had come to the conclusion that Norman slept in an aeroplane hangar at Luton Airport.

In the Studio.

Presenter   And so on February 22nd 1966, at Luton Airport ... (Film of a Nuclear Explosion).

In the Studio.

Presenter   Even the police began to sit up and take notice.

In a South London street Superintendent Harry 'Snapper' Organs addresses the camera, as passers-by move behind him.

Superintendent Organs   The Piranhas realised they had gone too far and that the hunt was on. They went into hiding. I decided on a subtle approach, viz. some form of disguise as the old helmet and boots are a bit of a giveaway. Luckily my years with Bristol Rep. stood me in good stead as I assumed a bewildering variety of disguises. I tracked them to Cardiff posing as the Reverend Smiler Egret. Hearing they'd gone back to London I assumed the identity of a pork butcher, Brian Stoats. On my arrival in London I discovered they had returned to Cardiff. I followed as Gloucester from *King Lear*. Acting on a hunch I spent several months in Buenos Aires as Blind Pew, returning through the Panama Canal as Ratty in *Toad of Toad Hall*. Back in Cardiff I relived my triumph as Sancho Panza (picture) in *Man of La Mancha* which the *Bristol Evening Post* described as 'a glittering performance of rare perception', although the *Bath Chronicle* was less than enthusiastic. In fact it gave me a right panning. I quote: 'As for the performance of Superintendent Harry "Snapper" Organs as Sancho Panza, the audience were bemused by his high-pitched Welsh accent and intimidated by his abusive ad-libs.' The *Western Daily News* said: 'Sancho Panza (Mr Organs) spoilt an otherwise impeccably choreographed rape scene by his unscheduled appearance and persistent cries of "what's all this, then?".'

Behind Superintendent Organs in the street, we notice a newspaper-seller receiving the latest batch of Evening Standards. He starts shouting.

Newspaper-Seller   Piranha Brothers Escape! Read all about it! Doug and Dinsdale on the loose!

The streets clear in a flash. Superintendent Organs runs up to the newspaper-seller and buys a copy. As he scans the front page, an enormous hedgehog appears, looking over the tops of the terraced houses in the street. The hedgehog calls quietly . . .

Spiny Norman   Dinsdale . . . Dins. . .dale?

(Original cast: Presenter *MV*; Mrs Simnel *Michael Palin*; Interviewer *Eric Idle*; Superintendent Harry 'Snapper' Organs *Terry Jones*; Vince Snetterton-Lewis *Graham Chapman*; Another Interviewer *Terry Jones*; Stig O'Tracy *Eric Idle*; Mrs O'Tracy *Graham Chapman*; Sid Flange *Terry Jones*; April Strong *MV*; Interviewer (again) *Eric Idle*; Dr Hardy-Ling *Graham Chapman*; Luigi Vercotti *Michael Palin*; Interviewer *Terry Jones*; and Spiny Norman)

Dead Parrot Skit

by MV and Graham Chapman;
'Monty Python's Flying Circus', 7 December 1969

Omitted by popular demand

Sources of the Skits
(Not a Skit)

Double Take
The 1962 Cambridge Footlights Revue; with Robert Atkins, Miriam Margoyles, Tim Brooke-Taylor, Nigel Brown, Humphrey Barclay, Graham Chapman, Tony Hendra, John Cleese and Alan George; musical direction by Hugh Macdonald; directed by Trevor Nunn.

Cambridge Circus
Original title 'A Clump of Plinths'; the 1963 Cambridge Footlights Revue, with Chris Stuart-Clark, Jo Kendall, Tony Buffery, Bill Oddie, David Hatch, Tim Brooke-Taylor and John Cleese; directed by Humphrey Barclay. Opened, under the title 'Cambridge Circus', at the New Arts Theatre, London, on 10 July 1963.

I'm Sorry, I'll Read That Again
Radio series on BBC Home Service/Radio 4. Preparatory series – three from 3 April 1964. First series – nine from 4 October 1965. Second series – thirteen from 14 March 1966. Third series – fourteen from 3 October 1966. Fourth series – fourteen from 23 March 1967. Fifth series – thirteen from 14 April 1968. Special – 26 December 1968. Sixth series – thirteen from 12 January 1969. Special – 25 December 1969. Seventh series – thirteen from 15 February 1970. Special – 31 December 1970. Eighth series – eight from 4 November 1973. With Tim Brooke-Taylor, Graeme Garden, John Cleese, Jo Kendall, David Hatch and Bill Oddie. Produced by Humphrey Barclay (Preparatory series and series 1–4), David Hatch and Peter Titheradge (series 5–8).

The Frost Report
Television series on BBC-1. Two series of thirteen programmes each, starting on 10 March 1966 and 6 April 1967. Principal performers David Frost, Ronnie Barker, Ronnie Corbett, John Cleese, Sheila Steafel, Julie Felix. The writing team included John Cleese, Graham Chapman, Frank Muir, Denis Norden, Marty Feldman, Keith Waterhouse, Willis Hall, Dick Vosburgh, Eric Idle, Michael Palin and Terry Jones.

At Last the 1948 Show
Television series for the then London ITV company, Associated–Rediffusion. Six programmes from 15 February 1967, and seven programmes from 26 September

1967. Written and performed by John Cleese, Graham Chapman, Tim Brooke-Taylor and Marty Feldman; also starring the lovely Aimi MacDonald.

Monty Python's Flying Circus
Television series for BBC-1. Thirteen programmes from 5 October 1969; thirteen programmes from 15 September 1970; thirteen programmes from 19 October 1972; and six programmes from 31 October 1974 under the title 'Monty Python'. Written and performed by John Cleese (not 4th series), Graham Chapman, Eric Idle, Michael Palin and Terry Jones, with animations by Terry Gilliam.

Monty Python's Matching Tie and Handkerchief
Gramophone record by the Monty Python team; Charisma CAS 1080 (UK), Arista AL 4039 (USA); also musicassette Charisma ZCCAS 1080, and 7208.558 (UK), and 8-track cartridge Charisma Y8CAS 1080, and 7749.558 (UK), Arista 8301–4039H (USA). First published 1973.

A Poke in the Eye with a Sharp Stick
Gala performances in aid of Amnesty International, given at Her Majesty's Theatre, London, on 1, 2 and 3 April 1976. The performers included John Cleese, Michael Palin, Terry Jones, Graham Chapman, Terry Gilliam, Peter Cook, Jonathan Miller, Alan Bennett, Jonathan Lynn, Eleanor Bron, Neil Innes, Barry Humphries, Tim Brooke-Taylor, Graeme Garden, Bill Oddie, John Fortune and John Bird.

The Mermaid Frolics
Gala Performances in aid of Amnesty International, given at the Mermaid Theatre, London, May 1977. Performers included Peter Cook, John Cleese, Connie Booth, Jonathan Miller and Terry Jones.

The Secret Policeman's Other Ball
Gala performances in aid of Amnesty International, given at the Theatre Royal, Drury Lane, London, on 9, 10, 11 and 12 September 1981. The performers included Rowan Atkinson, Jeff Beck, Alan Bennett, John Bird, Tim Brooke-Taylor, Jasper Carrott, Graham Chapman, Eric Clapton, John Cleese, Phil Collins, Billy Connolly, Donovan, John Fortune, Bob Geldorf, Barry Humphries, Neil Innes, Chris Langham, Griff Rhys-Jones, Alexei Sayle, Pamela Stephenson, Sting, John Wells and Victoria Wood. Directed by Ronald Eyre, assisted by John Cleese.

Monty Python's The Meaning of Life
Cinema film, 1983; produced by Celandine Films/The Monty Python Partnership for Universal. Producer John Goldstone; director Terry Jones; script John Cleese, Graham Chapman, Terry Gilliam, Michael Palin, Terry Jones, Eric Idle; animation director Terry Gilliam; photography Peter Hannan; editor Julian Doyle. Leading

players: Graham Chapman, John Cleese, Terry Gilliam, Eric Idle, Terry Jones, Michael Palin, Carol Cleveland, Simon Jones, Patricia Quinn, Judy Loe, Andrew MacLachlan, Mark Holmes, Valerie Whittington, Jennifer Franks, Imogen Bickford-Smith, Angela Mann, Peter Løvstrom, Victoria Plum, Anne Rosenfeld, George Silver.